BETTER BUSINESS LETTERS

JAMES M. REID, JR. and ANNE SILLECK

BETTER BUSINESS LETTERS

A Programed Book
to Develop Skill in Writing

SECOND EDITION

ADDISON-WESLEY PUBLISHING COMPANY

Reading, Massachusetts

Menlo Park, California · London · Amsterdam · Don Mills, Ontario · Sydney

ISBN 0-201-06327-1
BCDEFGHIJK-MA-798

CONTENTS

The back cover is perforated so that a portion can be torn off and used as an answer mask.

ACKNOWLEDGMENTS

We would like to thank Mr. E. J. Feeney, Assistant Vice President—Sales, Emery Air Freight Corporation; Mrs. Cecelia L. Baros, Assistant Training Specialist, Personnel Training, The Prudential Insurance Company of America; Mr. Robert Jud, Assistant Vice President, Skills Training Division, Bankers Trust Company; and Mr. Malcolm W. Warren, Manager of Training and Development, Questor Corporation, for their cooperation in administering the field test of our manuscript. Our thanks also go to the employees of the above firms who actually worked through the manuscript and gave us the data and comments with which to make revisions.

We would especially like to express our appreciation to Mrs. Linn Harding, whose attention to detail has helped us immensely in the production of this book.

Ridgefield, Conn.   **J.M.R.**
February 1978   **A.S.**

ABOUT THE SECOND EDITION

The second edition of *Better Business Letters* has been edited, updated, and expanded in order to improve its usefulness to trainers in business, industry, and government. Specifically, we have given the book a front-to-back editing in order to recognize the increased role that women and minorities are playing in all levels of business and government. To the extent of our awareness, we have tried to eliminate all constructions that may imply a sexist or ethnic bias.

We have also broken up Lesson 2 of the first edition into two separate lessons so that the book now consists of six lessons instead of five.

Additions to the first edition include an appendix on letter layout and other conventions and a diagnostic test to help trainers use the book more flexibly.

TO THE INSTRUCTOR

ABOUT THE BOOK

This programed book is designed to help your students develop skill in writing business letters. It is called a *program* because it uses programed instruction—a method of teaching that requires students to respond in writing while learning.

A quick glance at the material will show that it is different from that found in a conventional text. For one thing, the subject matter is presented in a series of small steps. Each step, called a *frame*, gives the students some information and then requires them to answer a question or practice a writing skill. After they have written their answer, they can uncover the correct answer and learn whether they are right or not. The whole process is much like conversing with an instructor who asks questions and tells the students if they have answered correctly.

This book has been developed in consultation with people in business and government and has been field-tested under conditions of actual use in four different organizations.

OBJECTIVES

Although we make no claim that this book "will teach your students how to write," we do believe that it will achieve the limited behavioral objectives it was designed to achieve. These objectives are listed below, lesson by lesson.

Lesson 1: Writing Concise Sentences. In this lesson students learn to . . .
  . . . detect and eliminate unnecessary words or phrases,
  . . . detect and revise wordy phrases and redundancies.

Lesson 2: Keeping Your Reader's Interest. In this lesson students learn to . . .
  . . . detect general words and to substitute more exact, specific ones,
  . . . distinguish between sentences written in the passive voice and those in the active voice,
  . . . convert passive sentences to active ones.

Lesson 3: Writing for Easy Reading. In this lesson students learn to . . .
  . . . use the appropriate link (*and, or, however,* etc.) to indicate the relationship between ideas,
  . . . detect errors in the use of parallelism and correct them.

Lesson 4: Being Natural, Courteous, and Personal. In this lesson students learn to . . .
    . . . detect inflated language and use simpler words,
    . . . detect archaic business expressions and substitute more modern ones,
    . . . use positive rather than negative language whenever possible,
    . . . achieve a more personal tone by using a generous sprinkling of "I," "you," and "we."

Lesson 5: The Start and the Finish. In this lesson students learn to . . .
    . . . write opening sentences which include an explanation of what the letter is about, the idea of most interest to the reader (if possible), and the date of the reader's letter (if applicable),
    . . . write closing sentences which do not contain the usual insincere clichés but which contain specific requests for action or summaries.

Lesson 6: Planning and Writing Your Letter. In this lesson students learn to . . .
    . . . detect and eliminate irrelevant ideas,
    . . . make a "laundry list" of ideas for organization,
    . . . salvage goodwill in a turn-down letter by using such devices as giving reasons before the actual turn-down, assuring careful consideration, or recommending positive alternatives.

HOW TO USE THIS BOOK

Anyone who must write business letters on the job will find this program useful. However, to achieve best results, the students should have at least a high school education.

The programed lessons can stand on their own as the sole means of instruction or they may be used in conjunction with other methods of instruction in a variety of learning situations.

The book is composed of an Introduction and six programed lessons, each accompanied by a Quiz. There are also an appendix on business-letter layout and other conventions and a Diagnostic Test.

The Diagnostic Test is included for those trainers who wish to use the book prescriptively. That is, they want their students to do only those lessons that will help them overcome specific weaknesses, thus saving them time. The various parts of the test are coordinated to each of the six lessons, so that if students do not score a passing grade in a certain part of the test, they may be referred to the corresponding lesson for instruction.

However, if you plan to require your students to work through the entire book, we recommend that you *do not* ask them to take the Diagnostic Test.

Important: If you plan to administer the Diagnostic Test and the Quizzes formally, be sure to tear pages 187 through 203 out of each copy of the book *before* you distribute it to students. These pages have the correct answers for scoring the test and quizzes.

Each lesson should take *about* an hour for a student to complete and each Quiz about one-half hour. However, individual students may vary from these times by as much as 50 percent.

To achieve best results, we recommend that the program be administered in six sessions, as outlined below.

	Approximate Study Time	
Diagnostic Test	30 minutes (optional)	
Orientation	15 minutes	
Introduction and Lesson 1	60 minutes	
Quiz — Lesson 1	30 minutes	
SESSION 1		105 minutes
Lesson 2	60 minutes	
Quiz — Lesson 2	30 minutes	
SESSION 2		90 minutes
Lesson 3	60 minutes	
Quiz — Lesson 3	30 minutes	
SESSION 3		90 minutes
Lesson 4	60 minutes	
Quiz — Lesson 4	30 minutes	
SESSION 4		90 minutes
Lesson 5	60 minutes	
Quiz — Lesson 5	30 minutes	
SESSION 5		90 minutes
Lesson 6	60 minutes	
Quiz — Lesson 6	30 minutes	
SESSION 6		90 minutes
TOTAL TIME		555 minutes or 9 hours 15 minutes

As you can see, each session lasts about an hour and a half. To be on the safe side, allow about two hours for each session. We recommend that one session be given each day for a total of six days. If you want to condense the time that the students work on the program, we recommend that you give one session in the morning and one in the afternoon, for a total of three days. *We strongly recommend that you do not ask the student to do more than two sessions in one day.*

We suggest that you provide a quiet place where the students can work without interruptions. Programed instruction requires much concentration and its effectiveness is dissipated if students are interrupted in the middle of a lesson. To administer the Diagnostic Test, simply ask the students to work through it in the back of their books, score it according to the answers on pages 187 to 193, and assign the appropriate lessons according to results.

Before the students start reading the Introduction, we suggest that you give them a brief orientation.

1. Explain that they are being given a training program that will help them develop skills for writing better business letters. Tell them they will be required to write the answers to questions as they work through the lessons. Be sure to emphasize that the program is not a test of their knowledge but is a method of instruction which includes self-testing.
2. Explain that when they finish a lesson, they will be given a Quiz to see how much they have learned. This will help motivate them to work conscientiously.
3. Ask them to write their answers carefully in the spaces provided in the book. If they make a mistake, they should understand why they were wrong before going on.
4. Tell them to work through the material at their own pace, to follow instructions, and not to hurry.

After the orientation, have them read the Introduction and begin work on Lesson 1. When they are finished with Lesson 1, have them take the Quiz for Lesson 1 in the back of the book. When they have finished, score the Quiz according to the correct answers provided in the back of the book. The test results should be discussed with the students.

Repeat this procedure for each lesson.

INTRODUCTION

Do you write good business letters?

That's not an easy question for most of us. Perhaps one way to find an answer is to ask yourself, "How does my business letter affect the person who reads it?"

Does it *confuse* the reader?

Valley National Bank
Valley City, New York 12183

August 8,

Mr. Elmer Liggens
Liggens' Drugstore
Main Street
Valley City, New York 12185

Dear Mr. Liggens:

With regard to reduction of your loan, to the extent permitted by, and as provided in, the terms of the loan agreement, consent by Valley National Bank is contingent upon a change of not less than 33-1/3% of the principal amount with a fixed maturity of...

OR . . .

Does it make the reader *angry*?

> The Judicial Insurance Company
> 11 Madison Avenue
> New York, New York 10016
>
> April 11,
>
> Mrs. Alice Jones
> 10 Black Rock Turnpike
> Atlanta, Georgia 30316
>
> Dear Mrs. James:
>
> Company policy dictates that we cannot
> possibly grant your request for a change
> of beneficiary for your husband's life
> insurance policy (#48-576-8372). In
> your letter of March 8, you claim that
> your husband gave you power of attorney,
> but...

OR . . .

Does it *bore* the reader?

> Management Consultants, Inc.
> 1186 Wilshire Boulevard
> Los Angeles, California 90016
>
> March 2,
>
> Mr. Thomas Cordero
> President
> Regent Manufacturing Company
> 1011 King Street
> Los Angeles, California 90046
>
> Dear Mr. Cordero:
>
> Enclosed herewith please find a presenta-
> tion of systematized concepts which may
> be of interest in the area of determining
> savings in production line efficiency--
> both as to the time factor and the
> monetary factor. Our firm is at the
> present time engaged in operating a
> functionalized system of reciprocal
> analysis which may achieve optimal re-
> sults on an integrated basis...

OR . . .

Does it do the job that you want it to?

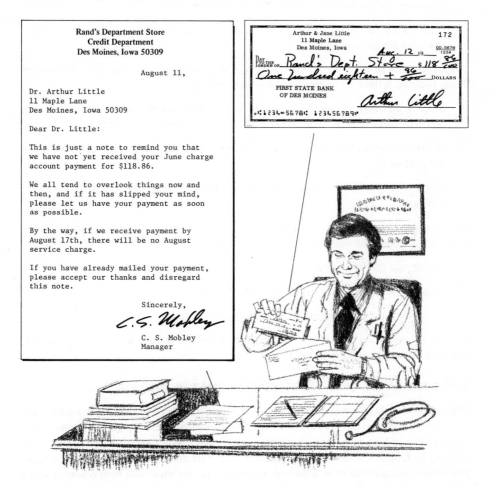

The point, of course, is that the best way to measure how well you write business letters is to see how well they accomplish their purposes. If a large percentage of your letters fail to do what you want them to—to affect the reader exactly as you intend—then you can probably use some improvement in your letter-writing skills.

THREE PURPOSES OF YOUR BUSINESS LETTERS

Many of your business letters have three basic purposes. The first and most obvious is to inform the reader—to communicate ideas and facts as accurately as possible from your mind to that of the reader. Thus, you will often find business letters with sentences such as the following:

I will be staying at the Clinton Hotel during the week of January 7.

We shipped 300,000 barrels of crude oil via the Erie Railroad on August 8. The shipment should arrive in Jersey City by the 24th.

I am happy to tell you that Regent Magazine *has decided to buy your article at the price we asked.*

A second purpose of many of your letters is to prod the reader into doing something. Thus, business letters often contain sentences such as these:

Since I am very much interested in exploring some of the ideas we discussed recently, please call me at 787-6852 and we can arrange a meeting.

If the shipment does not arrive by the 24th, send me a wire, and I will look into the problem.

Please sign the three copies of the contract and return them to me at the above address.

Not so obvious is the third purpose of most business letters—to make a good impression on the reader. Do many of your letters contain sentences such as the following?

Thank you for filling in and returning Form #308 so promptly.

I appreciate your efforts in behalf of Mr. Sears.

Please send the information to the following people: . . .

One of the purposes of such sentences is to create in the reader's mind a favorable image of the writer and his or her firm.

THE IMPORTANCE OF WRITING LETTERS THAT DO THE JOB

Most writers of business letters recognize the importance of informing the reader and of obtaining desired action because the achievement of these purposes is essential to the proper conduct of a firm's business. Letters are a major expense for many organizations. In fact, it has been estimated that they cost about $7.00 each and that some companies spend more than a million dollars a year on them. No firm wants to waste its communications dollars by sending letters that do not fully inform and do not get the action they should. Unclear or unpersuasive letters represent wasted time and money and often require expensive follow-up letters.

Equally as important as informing readers and getting proper action from them is making a good impression on them. Letters that do this are usually much more effective in accomplishing the other two objectives. Moreover, such letters often have two important side effects. First, they create a climate that helps your firm sell its goods or services. Perhaps your letters do not have anything to do with selling, but they can help sales by increasing the number of people who have a favorable image of your firm. Second, letters that build goodwill can help your career, and letters that do not can hinder it. For example, would you like your boss to receive something like the following?

June 10

Mrs. Ruth Klein
Manager
Adjustments Department
Connelly's Department Store
Boston, Massachusetts 02184

Dear Mrs. Klein:

I am writing to you about an extremely insulting letter which I just received from one of your employees, Mr. James Weed. I'm an adult and I expect to be so treated. Mr. Weed, however, seems to think I deserve a slap on the wrist because I thought your store should pay for repairs on a watch that I dropped. Mr. Weed may be right about the guarantee not covering breakage, but he doesn't have to be so snide about it.

You may be interested to know that I am taking the watch to a reputable jeweler to have it repaired at my own expense. I am also taking my business, which is considerable, to Allen's Department Store in the future.

Sincerely,

Mrs. Anne Turner

Or would you rather have her receive the following?

June 10

Mrs. Ruth Klein
Manager
Adjustments Department
Connelly's Department Store
Boston, Massachusetts 02184

Dear Mrs. Klein:

This letter is to authorize you to make the necessary repairs on my watch and to charge the expense to my account.

Also, I would like to say that I have never been turned down in such a nice way as Mr. James Weed did. I had originally asked your store to pay for the repairs under the guarantee. But Mr. Weed explained that the guarantee did not cover breakage. His letter was so courteous and clear that I could not help but accept defeat graciously.

In this day and age, when one is constantly bombarded by words written by apparent robots, Mr. Weed's letter came as a welcome relief.

Sincerely,

Mrs. Anne Turner

THE QUALITIES OF BETTER BUSINESS LETTERS

What should a good business letter be like? At a minimum, it should be—

CLEAR

CONCISE

WELL-ORGANIZED

NATURAL

COURTEOUS

PERSONAL

Let's discuss these qualities one by one. *Clarity*, of course, is essential if your letter is to achieve its purpose. The reader must understand exactly what your letter is trying to communicate. With this in mind, examine the following:

Dear Mr. Apdecker:

Contingent upon approval of those concerned, the remuneration of an individual partner for profit-sharing purposes will be deemed to be such proportion of the total available remuneration of all partners as the proportion of each partner's capital investment.

Now compare it with this:

Dear Mr. Apdecker:

If all three partners so agree, each partner will share in the profits in proportion to her or his initial capital investment. For instance, if Partner A invests $10,000 and Partners B and C invest $5,000 each, Partner A will receive one-half the profit while Partners B and C will receive one-quarter of the profit each.

This second version is much more likely to achieve its objective of informing the reader. Granted, very little writing is as muddy as the first example above, but if a letter leaves the reader any room for doubt, it may not accomplish its purposes.

Today, when most readers are inundated by a tremendous flow of written communication, *conciseness* is given high priority. People want to know what you have to say to them, as quickly as possible. This means saying it in the fewest words. It does not mean that your letters should be short or abrupt: a novel can be concise, while a single sentence can be unnecessarily wordy. Rather, conciseness is saying everything you have to say, without losing clarity or courtesy, in the fewest possible words.

Inconcise: It is hoped that word from Mr. Lewis in connection with the completion of the project will be received by us at an early date.   (25 words)

Concise: We hope to hear soon from Mr. Lewis about completing the project.
  (12 words, a saving of 13)

The concise sentence above says the same thing as the inconcise one in less than half the number of words. Imagine reading a letter filled with sentences such as the first one. You would probably be bored or irritated no matter how interesting the contents of the letter were.

Saying that a letter should be *well-organized* is saying that it should be thoroughly thought out. You should not sit down to think of what you will write but to write what you have thought. In other words, you can't expect your letter to be either clear or concise unless you have weeded out irrelevant ideas, chosen relevant ideas, and arranged them in an effective order. For example, suppose you are answering a letter of inquiry. In order to obtain the necessary information, you have to go to the company library and credit files, and you talk with several executives about the letter. Should you inform your reader of all this research? Probably not. The reader is primarily interested in the information you have obtained for him or her, not how you obtained it. Thus, if your letter opens, "Upon receiving your letter I went to the company library and also looked in our credit files . . . ," you would probably be writing a disorganized letter.

One of the most common faults of business-letter writers is their tendency to use archaic, pompous, or inflated language. This flowery writing style was acceptable almost 100 years ago. For instance, below is a letter from a book of models of business letters published in 1884. The book is called *Payne's Business Letter Writer and Book of Commercial Forms.* This example letter is from a fruit broker to a potential customer.

New York, May 1st, 1885
No. 50 Front St.

MESSRS. POPHAM, MAYO & CO.
No. 55 Beaver St., New York

GENTLEMEN: I beg to inform you that I have this day opened an office at the above number for transaction of business as broker in fruits and spices.

The knowledge and experience gained in 15 years, while in the employ of Messrs. Stark Bros. & Co., enables me to give you every assurance, while soliciting your countenance and support, that all orders entrusted to me for execution will receive my most careful attention.

Referring to Messrs. S. B. & Co., my late employers, as above, and Messrs. Dows, Cattlin & Co., of Front St.,

I remain, respectfully,

Your obedient servant,

Wording such as "I beg to inform you" and "in the employ of" was customary in the business world of long ago, but it is no longer appropriate for modern business writers. Nonetheless, such pompous, archaic usage still may be found in a surprisingly large number of business letters. For this reason, we emphasize that a business letter should be written in a *natural*, conversational style that does not call attention to itself at the expense of the ideas and facts you are trying to communicate.

A business letter must be not only natural but *courteous*. Courtesy to the reader is not just a matter of including such words as "please" and "thank you"—although they play an important part in being courteous—but it is also being positive rather than negative. Courtesy is saying, "We will try to have your toaster repaired by August 6," rather than, "We cannot have your toaster repaired until August 6." More important, courtesy is your attitude toward the reader. If you have a friendly, helpful feeling for the reader, your letter cannot help but reflect this attitude.

The last quality on our list is being *personal*. Your business letter should be a personal communication between two people rather than an impersonal notice from one statistic to another. This is particularly important today because as companies and other organizations become larger and more powerful, individuals become more sensitive to any suggestion that the organization or its representative does not *care*. So when you write business letters, you should strive to visualize your readers—to see them as people with feelings of their own and with problems and needs that are a little different from those of their fellows.

We believe, then, that these are the five qualities which make for better business letters.

ABOUT THIS BOOK

This book consists of six lessons which can help you gain skill in writing better business letters. Each lesson has been programed. That is, the material is presented in small steps called *frames*. Each frame presents some information and then requires you to answer a question or practice a writing skill. After you have written your answer, you can uncover the correct answer and learn whether you were right or not. This whole process is much like talking with an instructor who asks you questions and tells you when you are right.

Each frame is designed so that you will answer correctly most of the time—to help you learn. Programed instruction is *not* a test; it is a method of teaching which includes self-testing.

Now, a few words of advice:

1. Take your time. Read each frame carefully and work at your own pace. Each lesson should take about an hour, but don't worry if you take more or less time because we know that people learn at different rates and still may acquire the same amount of information and skill.

2. Each frame has enough space for you to write your answer directly on the page. When you get a wrong answer, reread the frame to understand why you were wrong.

3. A programed book, unlike a conventional text, cannot be scanned, crammed, or skipped. Nor should you begin in the middle of a lesson. Begin each lesson at the beginning and don't stop until you come to the end. Before you begin a lesson, be sure you have enough time to finish—about one hour.

4. You will need a pencil while working through the lessons.

As we mentioned in the Introduction, a concise sentence says what has to be said in the fewest number of words—without losing clarity or courtesy. This lesson will help you to write concise sentences by showing you how to recognize and eliminate some typical cases of business verbosity.

Tear off the mask from the back cover of this book and place it over this page so that the top edge lies just beneath the solid line below. Lower the mask slowly until you uncover a dotted line. Please do not go below this line until you have written your answer in the space provided.

UNNECESSARY WORDS AND PHRASES

Begin to study here.

1a

Some words and phrases that often crop up in business letters do nothing to carry the meaning of a sentence to the reader. Such unnecessary verbiage should be ruthlessly cut out with the stroke of a pen. Read the example below.

Please be advised that your payment arrived on June 13. (10 words)

Is the phrase "please be advised that" necessary to the meaning of this sentence?

Write *yes* or *no* in this space and then lower your mask to the next dotted line.

Stop here. . . . . Stop here

Check your answer with this correct answer.

no ◄─┘

1b

Rewrite the example sentence above so that it is concise. _____

_____

. . . .

Your payment arrived on June 13. (6 words, a saving of 4)

or

We received your payment on June 13. (7 words, a saving of 3)

Following the same procedure, continue to study here.

2

I wish to tell you that our meeting for April 10 has been postponed to April 16.

(17 words)

Cross out the phrase that can be eliminated from the above sentence without changing its meaning.

· ·

~~I wish to tell you that~~ our meeting for April 10 has been postoned to April 16.

(11 words, a saving of 6)

3

In each of the following sentences, cross out the unnecessary phrase.

    A. Our accountant is making a study along the lines of product costs.

    B. It happened that your electric iron did not arrive within the ninety-day warranty period.

    C. We have a high turnover rate because of the fact that our employees can readily find new jobs.

    D. We expect sales to rise about three or four percent next month.

· ·

    A. Our accountant is making a study ~~along the lines~~ of product costs.

    B. ~~It happened that~~ your electric iron did not arrive within the ninety-day warranty period.

    C. We have a high turnover rate because ~~of the fact that~~ our employees can readily find new jobs.

    D. We expect sales to rise ~~about~~ three or four percent next month. ("Three or four percent" is indefinite enough. "About" adds nothing.)

        or

        We expect sales to rise about three ~~or four~~ percent next month. ("About three" or "about four" is indefinite enough. "About three or four" is wordy.)

4

When you are expressing an opinion (as opposed to an objective statement of fact), it is often helpful to use such expressions as "I think . . . ," "It is my opinion that . . . ," or "We feel that . . . ." However, you are being wordy when you use such expressions as "I *personally* think . . ." because an opinion cannot be anything *but* personal.

In each of the following sentences, cross out the unnecessary word.

    A. We are looking for a receptionist with a pleasant sounding voice.

    B. I personally think that the present slump in prices is temporary.

    C. Mr. Manner, our former president, is located with American Motors.

    D. This new breed of mice can be effectively used for medical research purposes.

. . . .

    A. We are looking for a receptionist with a pleasant ~~sounding~~ voice.

    B. I ~~personally~~ think that the present slump in prices is temporary.

    C. Mr. Manner, our former president, is ~~located~~ with American Motors.

    D. This new breed of mice can be effectively used for medical research ~~purposes.~~

5

The following sentences may or may not contain one or more unnecessary words or phrases. Cross them out wherever they occur.

A. We think our laboratories are well equipped.

B. It's my personal opinion that the current trend in sales is unfavorable.

C. The Board of Directors plans to meet in about two or three weeks for further discussion along the lines of a merger with Regent Corporation.

D. Please be advised that machine-tool orders are up about six percent this month.

E. Please let us hear from you soon.

F. We are now located at 117 Springdale Road.

G. My partner, whose name is Mrs. McDonald, will be going to Europe for three weeks for purposes of a vacation.

. . . .

A. We think our laboratories are well equipped.

B. It's my ~~personal~~ opinion that the current trend in sales is unfavorable.

C. The Board of Directors plans to meet in ~~about~~ two or three weeks for further discussion ~~along the lines~~ of a merger with Regent Corporation.

   or

   The Board of Directors plans to meet in about two ~~or three~~ weeks for further discussion ~~along the lines~~ of a merger with Regent Corporation.

D. ~~Please be advised that~~ machine-tool orders are up about six percent this month.

E. Please let us hear from you soon.

F. We are now ~~located~~ at 117 Springdale Road.

G. My partner, ~~whose name is~~ Mrs. McDonald, will be going to Europe for three weeks for ~~purposes of~~ a vacation.

6a

Cross out all unnecessary words or phrases in the following paragraph.

I wish to tell you that an increase in prices is essential, which is due to the fact that there has been a rise in the cost of raw materials of about five or six percent. Moreover, our contract with the union expires July 31, and discussions along the lines of a new contract are already under way. I personally think the union will accept not less than a two percent increase.

. . . .

~~I wish to tell you that~~ an increase in prices is essential, ~~which is~~ due to ~~the fact that there has been~~ a rise in the cost of raw materials of ~~about~~ five or six percent (or: . . . of about five ~~or six~~ percent). Moreover, our contract with the union expires July 31, and discussions ~~along the lines~~ of a new contract are already under way. I ~~personally~~ think the union will accept not less than a two percent increase.

(An increase in prices is essential, due to a rise in the cost of raw materials of five or six percent. Moreover, our contract with the union expires July 31, and discussions of a new contract are already under way. I think the union will accept not less than a two percent increase.)

6b

Which of the above two versions of this paragraph, the original or the revised version, best presents the writer's message? _____

. . . .

the revised version   (It's 19 words shorter.)

WORDY PHRASES

7a

Some phrases are wordy, but one cannot remove them from a sentence without changing its meaning. Such phrases should be revised to be more concise. Look at the following example.

I am in receipt of your shipment of ten gross of #5 rubber bands.

What is a shorter way of saying "I am in receipt of?" _____

. . . .

I received, I have received

7b

I have here before me your letter of August 16.

Cross out the wordy phrase in the above sentence and write a shorter version over it.

. . . .

received
I ~~have here before me~~ your letter of August 16.
      ^

or

I have ~~here before me~~ your letter of August 16.

8

Please let us hear from you at an early date.

Cross out the wordy phrase in the above sentence and write a substitute word over your deletion.

. . . .

soon, shortly
Please let us hear from you ~~at an early date~~.
      ^

9a

    A. I will consider the plans, as stated above, carefully.

    B. I will consider the above plans carefully.

Which of these two sentences is more concise, A or B? _____

· ·

    B

9b

    The figures, as indicated below, may have a 10 percent margin of error.

Rewrite this sentence so that it is more concise. _____

_____

· ·

    The following figures may have a 10 percent margin of error.

    or

    The figures below may have a 10 percent margin of error.

Throughout the rest of this book you will be asked to rewrite many of our examples. We would like to emphasize that your revisions do not have to correspond word for word with our answers in order for you to be correct. Our answers represent what *we think* are the best revisions in the given circumstances. Perhaps, when you are comparing your answers with ours, you may think that yours are a little better or you may find that ours are a little more effective than yours. In any case, when you are trying to judge whether your answer is *correct*, ask yourself these two questions: "Have I done what the authors have asked me to do?" "Have I kept the exact meaning of the original?"

10

We are hiring an efficiency expert in order that he may discover the cause of our production lag.

To shorten this sentence, you would cross out the phrase "in order that he may" and substitute the single word "_____."

. . . .

to

to
We are hiring an efficiency expert ~~in order that he may~~ discover the cause of our production lag.
                                               ∧

11

My secretary recently wrote you in connection with our purchase of a used delivery truck.

The phrase "in connection with" should be replaced by the word "_____."

. . . .

about, regarding, concerning

about
My secretary recently wrote you ~~in connection with~~ our purchase of a used delivery truck.
                                           ∧

12

Below is a list of wordy phrases. In the space provided after each phrase, write one word that can be substituted for it.

A. in the normal course of procedure _____

B. as a consequence of _____

C. at the present time _____

D. in the immediate future _____

E. during the time that _____

F. for the purpose of _____

A. normally, usually, ordinarily
B. consequently, therefore, because of, due to
C. presently, now, currently
D. soon
E. while, when
F. to, for

13

Some of the following sentences contain wordy or unnecessary phrases. Cross them out and, when required, write your revision.

A. We will consider your proposal at an early date.

B. We will answer you as soon as possible.

C. We are considering the suggestion contained in your letter of October 23.

D. The suggestions, as stated above, were received from union employees.

E. In the usual course of business we serve in the neighborhood of five hundred people a day.

F. Please distribute this memo through the usual channels.

. . . .

                       soon, shortly

A. We will consider your proposal ~~at an early date~~.

B. We will answer you as soon as possible.

C. We are considering the suggestion ~~contained~~ in your letter of October 23.

      above

D. The suggestions~~, as stated above,~~ were received from union employees.

    Usually, normally   about

E. ~~In the usual course of business~~ we serve ~~in the neighborhood of~~ five hundred people a day.

F. Please distribute this memo through the usual channels.

14

On the left below is a list of wordy phrases. Match each one with a more concise substitute by writing the appropriate letter next to the appropriate number.

_____	1. in the immediate future	A.	to
_____	2. I am in receipt of		
_____	3. as a consequence of	B.	I received
_____	4. at an early date	C.	following
_____	5. I have here before me		
_____	6. as stated below	D.	while
_____	7. during the time that	E.	soon
_____	8. for the purpose of		
_____	9. at the present time	F.	now
_____	10. in connection with		
_____	11. in order that he may	G.	therefore
_____	12. in the neighborhood of	H.	usually
_____	13. in the normal course of procedure		
		I.	about

. . . .

1. E
2. B
3. G
4. E
5. B
6. C
7. D
8. A
9. F
10. I
11. A
12. I
13. H

15

Revise the following paragraph by crossing out the wordy phrases and writing in shorter versions.

I have here before me your letter of May 16 requesting delivery of your order in the immediate future. As a consequence of this, I have sent your shipment via air-freight instead of by rail as we would in the normal course of procedure.

. . . .

       received   immediate, early

I ~~have here before me~~ your letter of May 16 requesting delivery of your order ~~in~~

                            Consequently, Therefore

~~the immediate future.~~ ~~As a consequence of this,~~ I have sent your shipment via air-

                      normally

freight instead of by rail as we would ~~in the normal course of procedure.~~

(I received your letter of May 16 requesting immediate delivery of your order. Consequently, I have sent your shipment via air-freight instead of by rail as we normally would.)

16a

WM. HARDCASTLE CO.
1670 Main Street

January 24

Frank Dixon
Partner
Appleby, Dixon & Pearsall—Civil Engineers
2930 Market Street

Dear Mr. Dixon:

Please be advised that I have carefully considered your letter of January 22, in which you outline in some detail a plan for the matter of automating our plant located at 26th Street. As a consequence of this, I have given your plan into the hands of my assistant, whose name is John Masters, in order that he may determine whether or not it has practical application for our purposes from a financial viewpoint.

Mr. Masters will be in touch with you by phone by about the first or second of April with regard to his determination. If it so happens that you wish to consult us at an earlier date along the lines of his preliminary findings, I am personally sure he will be glad to answer any of your questions in connection with this matter.

Sincerely,

William Hardcastle

Is the above letter an example of concise writing? _____

. . . .

no

16b

Cross out any unnecessary or wordy phrases and write in appropriate revisions where required.

. . . .

~~Please be advised that~~ I have carefully considered your letter of January 22, in

detailed
which you outline ~~in some detail~~ a ∧ plan for ~~the matter of~~ automating our plant

Consequently
~~located~~ at 26th Street. ~~As a consequence of this~~, I have given your plan ~~into the~~

to   to
~~hands of~~ my assistant, ~~whose name is~~ John Masters, ~~in order that he may~~ deter-
   ∧   ∧

its financial practicality (or) whether it is financially practical.
mine ∧ ~~whether or not it has practical application for our purposes from a finan-~~

~~cial viewpoint~~.

phone   April 1 or 2
Mr. Masters will ~~be in touch with~~ you ~~by phone~~ by ~~about the first or second of~~
                              ∧   ∧

regarding, about
~~April with regard to~~ his determination. If ~~it so happens that~~ you wish to consult
   ∧

sooner   about
us ~~at an earlier date along the lines of~~ his preliminary findings, I am ~~personally~~
      ∧   ∧

sure he will be glad to answer any of your questions ~~in connection with this~~

~~matter~~.

16c

WM. HARDCASTLE CO.
1670 Main Street

January 24

Frank Dixon
Partner
Appleby, Dixon & Pearsall—Civil Engineers
2930 Market Street

Dear Mr. Dixon:

I have carefully considered your letter of January 22, in which you outlined a detailed plan for automating our plant at 26th Street. Consequently, I have given your plan to my assistant, John Masters, to determine its financial practicality.

Mr. Masters will phone you on April 1 or 2 regarding his determination. If you wish to consult us sooner about his preliminary findings, he will be glad to answer any of your questions.

Sincerely,
William Hardcastle

Is the above revised letter an example of concise writing? _____

. . . .

yes   (It's 66 words shorter.)

REDUNDANT WORDS AND PHRASES

17a

Phrases that say the same thing twice are redundant. Consider the following sentence:

The basic fundamentals of our new marketing scheme are outlined in the enclosed brochure.

Fundamentals are by definition basic. Therefore, the revision should be:

The basics of our new marketing scheme are outlined in the enclosed brochure.

or

The fundamentals of our new marketing scheme are outlined in the enclosed brochure.

Circle the redundant words in the following sentence.

It is the same identical approach we used last year.

· ·

It is the (same identical) approach we used last year.

17b

Using the answer above, cross out the unnecessary word in the circled phrase.

· ·

same ~~identical~~   or   ~~same~~ identical

18

Circle the redundant phrase in the following sentence and cross out the unnecessary word.

Because of this recent discovery, we must start our research over again.

· ·

Because of this recent discovery, we must start our research (~~over~~ again.)

or

Because of this recent discovery, we must start our research (over ~~again.~~)

19a

Circle the redundant phrases in the following sentence.

Each and every American should be taught the basic fundamentals of the law.

. . . .

(Each and every) American should be taught the (basic fundamentals) of the law.

19b

Now rewrite this sentence by filling in the blanks.

_____ American should be taught the _____ of the law.

. . . .

Each (or Every)
basics (or fundamentals)

20a

Circle all the redundant phrases in the following paragraph.

Much preliminary thought and consideration has gone into arranging our sales conference this year. The executive committee has decided that the right and proper approach to this conference should be to develop a polite and courteous attitude in our salesmen. A full and complete outline of the proposed agenda is enclosed.

. . . .

Much preliminary (thought and consideration) has gone into arranging our sales conference this year. The executive committee has decided that the (right and proper) approach to this conference should be to develop a (polite and courteous) attitude in our salesmen. A (full and complete) outline of the proposed agenda is enclosed.

20b

In each of the redundant phrases above, one word is sufficient to express the meaning. Rewrite the paragraph by filling in the blank spaces.

Much preliminary _____ has gone into arranging our sales conference this year. The executive committee has decided that the _____ _____ approach to this conference should be to develop a _____ attitude in our salesmen. A _____ outline of the proposed agenda is enclosed.

. . . .

thought (or consideration)   polite (or courteous)
right (or proper)   full (or complete)

21

Each of the following sentences contains a redundant phrase. Circle each of the redundant phrases and cross out the unnecessary word.

    A. The true facts speak for themselves.

    B. We are looking for a warehouse to rent because our stockrooms are too small in size to hold our expanded inventory.

    C. All applicants for this position must show due proof of age.

    D. We first began looking for a new site in 1978.

    E. The receipt will then be returned back to you.

. . . .

    A. The (~~true~~ facts) speak for themselves.

    B. We are looking for a warehouse to rent because our stockrooms are too (small ~~in size~~) to hold our expanded inventory.

    C. All applicants for this position must show (~~due~~ proof) of age.

    D. We (~~first~~ began) looking for a new site in 1978.

    E. The receipt will then be (returned ~~back~~) to you.

22

The following letter is riddled with no less than eleven redundancies. Circle each one and cross out the unnecessary word or words.

Gentlemen and Sirs:

We have just recently developed a new and original product which we plan to introduce to the market in late spring or early summer. After much thought and deliberation, we have decided to launch an all-out, no-holds-barred advertising and promotional campaign to acquaint the public with our product before it comes out. As your firm has a reputation for being both reliable and trustworthy, we would like to sit down and consult with you on ways and means of best marketing our product.

Cordially and courteously yours,

. . . .

(Gentlemen ~~and Sirs~~:)

We have (~~just~~ recently) developed a (new ~~and original~~) product which we plan to introduce to the market in (late spring ~~or early summer~~.) After much (thought ~~and deliberation,~~) we have decided to launch an (all-out, ~~no-holds-barred~~) (advertising ~~and promotional~~) campaign to acquaint the public with our product before it comes out. As your firm has a reputation for being (~~both~~ reliable ~~and trustworthy,~~) we would like to (~~sit down and~~ consult) with you on (ways ~~and means~~) of best marketing our product.

(Cordially ~~and courteously~~) yours,

REVIEW

23

In this lesson you have learned how to delete unnecessary words, revise wordy phrases, and eliminate redundancies. The following sentence contains an example of each of these mistakes. Revise it.

Please be advised that your order for twenty-one barrels of commercial grade oil has been received and duly noted and shipment has been arranged for the immediate future. (29 words)

. . . .

~~Please be advised that~~ your order for twenty-one barrels of commercial grade oil

immediate

has been received ~~and duly noted~~ and ⋀ shipment has been arranged ~~for the imme-

diate future.~~ (19 words, a saving of 10)

or

Immediate shipment of your order for twenty-one barrels of commercial grade oil has been arranged. (16 words, a saving of 13)

or

We have arranged to ship your order for twenty-one barrels of commercial grade oil immediately. (16 words, a saving of 13)

24

Each of the following sentences contains one or more verbosities. Revise them.

A. During the time that I am on vacation, my assistant, whose name is Mrs. Clare Winters, will be in charge of the Claims Division.

B. Because of the fact of recent discoveries, we shall have to begin our planning over again.

C. As a consequence of this, please let us hear from you at an early date.

D. In the normal course of procedure, we try to increase sales in the neighborhood of about 5 or 6 percent a year.

· ·

     While, When
A. ~~During the time that~~ I am on vacation, my assistant, ~~whose name is~~ Mrs. Clare
        ∧
Winters, will be in charge of the Claims Division.

B. Because of ~~the fact of~~ recent discoveries, we shall have to begin our planning over ~~again.~~

     Therefore, Consequently   soon
C. ~~As a consequence of this,~~ please let us hear from you ~~at an early date.~~
        ∧   ∧

     Usually, Normally, Generally
D. ~~In the normal course of procedure,~~ we try to increase sales ~~in the neighbor-~~
              ∧
~~hood of~~ about 5 ~~or 6~~ percent a year.

25a

Revise the following letter to make it more concise.

EMPIRE DECORATORS, INC.
1621 Broadway

February 16

Mr. Harold Gold
Stasson & Gold, Inc.
16 Spring Street

Dear Mr. Gold:

It happens that I have just now received your letter inviting our bid for the purpose of remodeling your offices located at 16 Spring Street. As a consequence of this, our estimate is not based on a full and complete examination of the premises as we would prefer in the normal course of procedure. For example, although we have included a figure for painting costs for the extent of 1,672 square feet of wall area, we have not included a figure for any preliminary or prerequisite costs that may be involved in preparing the walls for painting due to the fact that their condition is an unknown factor.

However, in order that you may gain a more realistic picture of this matter, you may add about 10 or 12 percent to our bid to cover any additional or extra costs.

Sincerely,

. . . .

EMPIRE DECORATORS, INC.
1621 Broadway

February 16

Mr. Harold Gold
Stasson & Gold, Inc.
16 Spring Street

Dear Mr. Gold:

~~It happens that~~ I have just ~~now~~ received your letter inviting our bid for ~~the~~

Consequently
~~purpose of~~ remodeling your offices ~~located~~ at 16 Spring Street. ~~As a consequence~~
~~of this,~~ our estimate is not based on a ~~full and~~ complete examination of the

normally
premises as we would prefer ~~in the normal course of procedure.~~ For example,

although we have included a figure for painting costs for ~~the extent of~~ 1,672

square feet of wall area, we have not included a figure for any preliminary ~~or~~

~~prerequisite~~ costs that may be involved in preparing the walls for painting ~~due~~

as, because, since
~~to the fact that~~ their condition is ~~an~~ unknown ~~factor.~~

to
However, ~~in order that you may~~ gain a more realistic picture ~~of this matter,~~ you

may add ~~about~~ 10 or 12 percent to our bid to cover any additional ~~or extra~~ costs.

Sincerely,

25b

The letter should now read:

Dear Mr. Gold:

I have just received your letter inviting our bid for remodeling your offices at 16 Spring Street. Consequently, our estimate is not based on a complete examination of the premises as we normally would prefer. For example, although we have included a figure for painting costs for 1,672 square feet of wall area, we have not included a figure for any preliminary costs that may be involved in preparing the walls for painting as their condition is unknown.

However, to gain a more realistic picture, you may add 10 or 12 percent to our bid to cover any additional costs.

As a reader, which of these two versions of the letter, the original or the revised, creates a better impression of the company? _____

. . . .

the revised version

This is the end of Lesson 1. Now turn to page 169 and take the Quiz for Lesson 1.

This lesson can help you keep your reader's interest by teaching the use of *specific words* and *active sentences.*

Specific Words: As mentioned in the Introduction, clarity is always a prerequisite for the business letter that best does the job. Thus it is extremely important that you choose words that most exactly express your meaning. You may have a very clear and precise thought that you wish the reader to understand, but if you do not choose the right words to express it, the reader may misunderstand—with unpleasant consequences for yourself and your organization.

Sometimes, business writers have a tendency to use general words when *specific words* are needed. These general words are often clichés and are usually plugged in without too much thought. Below is a sentence containing two general words which should be replaced with more specific ones.

> Our production manager, Mr. Calhoun, feels that if your firm adopts the Merckle Computer System, it will have a *measurable effect* on production efficiency.

This sentence tells us very little because the writer has used two general words, "measurable effect." What does "measurable" really tell us? Will the effect on production efficiency be large, small, or something in between? All such effects are presumably "measurable." And what about "effect" itself? Will production be beneficially or detrimentally influenced by the computer system? These questions go unanswered because the two words are too general to convey anything but the vaguest of concepts.

Granted, the writer of the above sentence could make up for its lack of clarity in other sentences, but he would then probably be guilty of wordiness. For a sentence that is unclear is often inconcise.

The first part of the upcoming lesson will give you some practice in choosing specific words to make meaning clearer.

Active Sentences: The second part of the lesson will show you how to make your sentences active, that is, to write them so that the verb is in the active voice. If your letters contain many active sentences, they will be not only more concise but more lively and interesting. To demonstrate this point, we present below the first parts of two news articles—one with many active sentences and one with many passive sentences.

(Passive)

COLLISION REPORTED ON MAIN STREET

Shortly after 3 p.m. yesterday, at the intersection of Main and Farnum Streets, there was an accident between James P. O'Hara's late model sedan and a pickup truck, driven by Mr. A. C. Jones. A load of watermelons was being carried by the truck. These watermelons were deposited by the impact on the sidewalk in front of Dealy's Drugstore. A cry of "free watermelons!" was immediately set up by a small boy.

(Active)

CAR AND TRUCK COLLIDE ON MAIN STREET

Shortly after 3 p.m. yesterday, at the intersection of Main and Farnum Streets, Mr. James P. O'Hara's late model sedan collided with Mr. A.C. Jones's pickup truck. The impact deposited the truck's load of watermelons on the sidewalk in front of Dealy's Drugstore. A small boy immediately set up a cry of "free watermelons!"

The second paragraph is shorter and more lively, primarily because all the sentences are active, while the first one has too many passive sentences.

SPECIFIC WORDS

1a

Suppose you are a regional sales manager of your firm, and you have recently instituted a successful incentive program for your sales people. You are now writing to your boss to tell her about it. Which of the following sentences is most likely to arouse her interest? _____ least likely? _____

    A.   The incentive program proved worthwhile.

    B.   The incentive program was effective in raising sales.

    C.   The incentive program raised sales by 40 percent in three weeks.

. . . .

C, A

1b

Which of the above sentences is the most specific? _____ the least? _____

. . . .

    C, A

2a

Which of the following words is most specific? _____

    A. communication

    B. letter

    C. message

    D. thought

. . . .

    B. letter

2b

Suppose you have received a complimentary letter from a customer and wish to acknowledge it. Fill in the best of the words A–D above in the following sentence:

    I received your _____ today and wish to thank you for writing us about

    the additional uses you've found for our product.

. . . .

    letter

3a

Which of the following verbs is most specific? _____

    A. to phone

    B. to contact

    C. to be (in touch with)

. . . .

    A. to phone

3b

Which of the following sentences is most informative? _____

    A. I'll contact you on Tuesday.

    B. I'll phone you on Tuesday.

    C. I'll be in touch with you on Tuesday.

. . . .

    B

4

    to send

    to forward

    to mail

Write in the most specific of the above three verbs in the following sentence:

    As you suggested, I will _____ our Fall Catalogue to you as soon as we

    receive it from our printers.

. . . .

    mail

5a

Cross out the uninformative, general word in the following sentence:

Dr. Small's lecture was worthwhile.

. . . .

Dr. Small's lecture was ~~worthwhile~~.

5b

Of the following words, circle the *word or words* that are more specific than "worthwhile."

valuable

informative

good

witty

. . . .

valuable

(informative)

good

(witty)   (Dr. Small's lecture was witty, informative, enlightening, stimulating, etc.)

6

In each of the following sentences cross out the vague word and write in something more specific.

    A. A copy of our report went to you this morning.

    B. Please communicate with us no later than Friday.

    C. Please excuse the delay in answering your message but I just returned from vacation.

. . . .

                                       was mailed, was sent by parcel post, etc.

    A. A copy of our report ~~went~~ to you this morning.
                                   Λ

                call, write, etc.

    B. Please ~~communicate with~~ us no later than Friday.
              Λ

                                   letter, note, etc.

    C. Please excuse the delay in answering your ~~message~~ but I just returned from
                                            Λ
       vacation.

SPECIFIC VERBS

7

In each of the following pairs of verbs, circle the more specific one.

to cable	—	to contact
to send	—	to deliver
to accomplish	—	to build
to change	—	to effect
to travel	—	to fly
to react	—	to reply
to cook (food)	—	to prepare (food)
to classify	—	to separate
to refund	—	to pay
to manufacture	—	to produce

. . . .

(to cable)	—	to contact
to send	—	(to deliver)
to accomplish	—	(to build)
(to change)	—	to effect
to travel	—	(to fly)
to react	—	(to reply)
(to cook (food))	—	to prepare (food)
(to classify)	—	to separate
(to refund)	—	to pay
(to manufacture)	—	to produce

8a

One of the best ways to invigorate your sentences is to use specific verbs. Sentences with specific verbs are not only clearer but more concise. For example, the following sentence has a general verb.

The consultant *effected* a complete overhaul of the organization of the office.

This is nct a very bad sentence, but it can be improved by using a more specific verb than "eff.cted." Note that the real action that Mr. Jones performed is hiding in the noun, "overhaul." If we convert this "action noun" to an "action verb" and substitute that verb for "effected," we come up with:

The consultant completely *overhauled* the organization of the office.

This sentence is three words shorter and five times as vigorous as the first one.

Recovery of lost articles can be accomplished by applying at the manager's office.

Underline the verb in the above sentence.

· ·

Recovery of lost articles <u>can be accomplished</u> by applying at the manager's office.

8b

Recovery of lost articles <u>can be accomplished</u> by applying at the manager's office.

Is this verb vague or specific?_____

. . . .

vague

8c

Now circle the word in the above sentence in which the action of the sentence is hiding.

. . . .

(Recovery) of lost articles <u>can be accomplished</u> by applying at the manager's office.

8d

Now rewrite this sentence by replacing the verb "accomplished" with a more specific one.

Lost articles can be _____ by applying at the manager's office.

. . . .

recovered

9a

Underline the verb in the following sentence:

We achieved success in raising production.

. . . .

We <u>achieved</u> success in raising production.

9b

Circle the word or words in which the specific action of this sentence is hidden.

. . . .

We achieved (success) in (raising) production.

9c

Now rewrite the sentence by filling in the verb.

We _____ in raising production.

. . . .

succeeded

9d

Rewrite the sentence by using the other action as the verb. _____

_____

. . . .

We (successfully) *raised* production.

10a

As shown in the previous frame, there are often several ways that an idea can be expressed. The way you express your ideas should always reflect your own style and personality. However, some faults should be avoided because they tend to make your writing less clear and concise.

Below are four sentences saying the same thing. Which one needs to be rewritten?

_____

    A.   You can expect delivery of your order before Wednesday.

    B.   Your order will be delivered before Wednesday.

    C.   Delivery of your order will be effected before Wednesday.

    D.   We will deliver your order before Wednesday.

· ·

    C.   Delivery of your order will be effected before Wednesday.

10b

Using our answer above, cross out the verb and circle the word in which action is hiding.

· ·

    C. (Delivery) of your order ~~will be effected~~ before Wednesday.

10c

Rewritten, the sentence would now resemble sentence B above. However, could you have used sentences A or D just as well? _____

· ·

    yes

11a

In each of the following sentences, cross out the vague verb and circle the word in which the action is hidden.

    A. A price increase on all replacement parts was effected last month.

    B. We sustained a loss of almost $40,000 in yesterday's fire.

    C. We suggest that automation of the 51st Street plant be accomplished during the slack summer months.

    D. Registration of claims will be accepted at the offices of Harrison & Jones.

. . . .

    A. A price (increase) on all replacement parts ~~was effected~~ last month.

    B. We ~~sustained~~ a (loss) of almost $40,000 in yesterday's fire.

    C. We suggest that (automation) of the 51st Street plant ~~be accomplished~~ during the slack summer months.

    D. (Registration) of claims ~~will be accepted~~ at the offices of Harrison & Jones.

11b

Now rewrite each of the above sentences by filling in the verb:

    A. Prices on all replacement parts _____ last month.

    B. We _____ almost $40,000 in yesterday's fire.

    C. We suggest that the 51st Street plant be _____ during the slack summer months.

    D. Claims can be _____ at the offices of Harrison & Jones.

. . . .

    A. increased, rose

    B. lost

    C. automated

    D. registered

12

The following paragraph is a model of vague verbosity. To revise it, first cross out any vague words and then circle any words in which the action of a sentence is hiding. Then write in your corrections over the crossed out words.

> In response to your communication of June 19, let me first make known my congratulations on your proposal to achieve a streamlining of our accounting department. The plan seems both worthwhile and workable. I am of the opinion, therefore, that your plan should be introduced for consideration by our committee at their next meeting, and I will be in touch with you when they effect a decision to adopt it or not.

. . . .

In response to your ~~communication~~ of June 19, let me first ~~make known my~~
  ↑ letter, phone call, etc.   ↑ congratulate you

(congratulations) on your proposal to ~~achieve a~~ (streamlining) ~~of~~ our accounting
                                          ↑ streamline

department. The plan seems ~~both worthwhile and~~ workable. I ~~am of the~~ (opinion,)
                                                              ↑ think

therefore, that your plan should be ~~introduced for~~ (consideration) by our com-
                                       ↑ considered

mittee at their next meeting, and I will ~~be in touch with~~ you when they ~~effect a~~
                                            ↑ call, write, etc.   ↑ decide

(decision) to adopt it or not.

This paragraph should now read:

> In response to your letter of June 19, let me first congratulate you on your proposal to streamline our accounting department. The plan seems workable. I think, therefore, that your plan should be considered by our committee at their next meeting, and I will call you when they decide to adopt it or not.

ACTIVE SENTENCES

13a

Jones wrote the letter.

In active sentences, the *subject* is the *doer* of the action. What word is the subject of the above sentence? _____

. . . .

Jones

13b

The above sentence is (an active/a passive) sentence.

Circle your choice.

. . . .

an active sentence

(Because "Jones" is both the subject and the doer of the action, the above sentence is an active sentence; that is, its verb is in the active voice.)

13c

The letter was written by Jones.

What word is the subject of the above sentence? _____

. . . .

letter

13d

In the above sentence, the word "letter" is (the doer of the action/acted upon).

. . . .

acted upon

13e

Therefore, the above sentence is (an active/a passive) sentence.

. . . .

a passive sentence

14a

    A. The report of preliminary findings was delivered by John Bonadio.

    B. We expect to publish our annual report in late June.

Underline the subjects of each of the above sentences.

. . . .

    A. The <u>report</u> of preliminary findings was delivered by John Bonadio.

    B. <u>We</u> expect to publish our annual report in late June.

14b

Using our answer above, circle the doers of the action in each of the above sentences.

. . . .

    A. The <u>report</u> of preliminary findings was delivered by (John Bonadio.)

    B. (<u>We</u>) expect to publish our annual report in late June.

14c

Which sentence is active, A or B? _____

. . . .

B

15a

Circle the doer of the main action in each of the following sentences.

    A. The turret lathe in the front row was repaired by Peabody, Inc.

    B. It is thought by some that our gold reserves are dangerously low.

    C. We need to revamp our advertising program in time for next season.

    D. Nobody can foresee what the stock market will do these days.

    E. A new discount rate will be announced by the Federal Reserve Board next month.

. . . .

    A. The turret lathe in the front row was repaired by (Peabody, Inc.)

    B. It is thought by (some) that our gold reserves are dangerously low.

    C. (We) need to revamp our advertising program in time for next season.

    D. (Nobody) can foresee what the stock market will do these days.

    E. A new discount rate will be announced by the (Federal Reserve Board) next month.

15b

Which of the above sentences are active? _____

. . . .

    C and D

15c

Make the passive sentences above active by filling in the subject and verb in the following:

A. _____ _____ the turret lathe in the
        SUBJECT   VERB

   front row.

B. _____ _____ that our gold reserves
        SUBJECT   VERB

   are dangerously low.

E. _____ _____ a new discount rate
        SUBJECT   VERB

   next month.

. . . .

A. Peabody, Inc.   repaired
   _____   _____
        SUBJECT   VERB

B. Some   think
   _____   _____
        SUBJECT   VERB

E. The Federal Reserve Board   will announce
   _____   _____
        SUBJECT   VERB

(Notice how much shorter and more direct the active versions are.)

16a

A. The meeting came to order.

B. The case was closed.

In which sentence is the subject the doer of the action? _____

. . . .

A

16b

Which sentence is the active sentence? _____

. . . .

A

16c

Sentence B above is a passive sentence. Is the doer of the action present in the sentence? _____

. . . .

no

16d

Think up a plausible doer of the action and rewrite sentence B so that it is active.

_____

_____
. . . .

The police (the F.B.I., the investigator, etc.) closed the case.

17a

As you can see from our last example, the doer of the action is not always present in a passive sentence. However, this will not be a problem in your own letters because you will of course know who or what is performing the action of the sentence. Suppose you have written the following:

A letter was received today from Nome, Alaska.

Is this sentence active or passive? _____

. . . .

passive

17b

A letter was received today from Nome, Alaska.

Think up a doer of the action for the above sentence and make it active.

· ·

I (We, Mr. Jones, Someone, etc.) received a letter from Nome, Alaska today.

18a

Sometimes, a sentence is passive and its verb is too general. For example:

Agreement on the overtime-wage issue was reached last month by Local 201 of the Iron Workers Union and the management of Teco Corporation.

Circle the word in the above sentence in which specific action is hidden.

· ·

(Agreement) on the overtime-wage issue was reached last month by Local 201 of the Iron Workers Union and the management of Teco Corporation.

18b

Now revise the sentence by making it active and by using the specific action as the verb. _____

· ·

Local 201 of the Iron Workers Union and the management of Teco Corporation agreed (reached an agreement) on the overtime-wage issue last month.

19a

Revise the following sentences so that they are active. If necessary, use a more specific verb and/or make up a plausible doer of the action.

A comprehensive report on marketing techniques has been prepared by F. Gonzales Associates.

_____

_____

· ·

F. Gonzales Associates has prepared a comprehensive report on marketing techniques.

19b

An improved method of transporting our natural gas products is necessary to meet the increased demand in the suburbs.

_____

_____

_____

· ·

We (Our firm, etc.) must improve our methods of transporting our natural gas products to meet the increased demand in the suburbs.

19c

A neutralization of the corrosive acids in the bottom of the mixing vat is accomplished by this new, white compound.

. . . .

This new, white compound neutralizes the corrosive acids in the bottom of the mixing vat.

20

Below is a letter written by a paper products manufacturer in reply to a customer who has complained that some adding machine tape, which he bought from a local wholesaler, was damaged. He has asked the manufacturer to replace the order.

On the next page, revise this letter so that the sentences are active.

PARAGON PAPER PRODUCTS, INC.
16 Faraday Avenue

June 19

Mr. George E. Jackson
Office Supply Manager
Regent Insurance Company
11 Wilson Street

Dear Mr. Jackson:

My apology is rendered to you for the trouble you have had with your order for adding machine tape. However, it is my advice that a complaint be filed by you with your local wholesaler because it appears that the damage described by you was caused by his mishandling. Perhaps the carton containing the tape was inadvertently slashed by his stockboy. If so, the replacement of your order would have to be accomplished by the wholesaler.

However, if the name of your supplier is furnished us, an inquiry on your behalf will be gladly sent him from this office.

Sincerely,

Your revision of the above letter does not have to compare word for word with ours below. However, it should have a majority of active sentences.

Dear Mr. Jackson:

I apologize to you for the trouble you have had with your order for adding machine tape. However, *I advise* you to file a complaint with your local whole-saler because it appears that his *mishandling caused* the damage *you described.* Perhaps his *stockboy inadvertently slashed* the carton containing the tape. If so, your *wholesaler would have to replace* your order.

However, if *you will furnish* us with the name of your wholesaler, *we* (this office) *will gladly send* him an inquiry in your behalf.

Sincerely,

This is the end of Lesson 2. Now turn to page 171 and take the Quiz for Lesson 2.

Your writing should be as easy to read as you can make it. This lesson covers two writing devices which can help make your reader's job easier and which therefore increase the likelihood that you will be completely understood. These devices are called *links* and *parallelism*.

Links: Links are words which serve readers in much the same way as road signs serve the drivers of cars. They tell them what to expect and thus make their trips safer and smoother. The first section of Lesson 3 will show you how to connect your ideas by using links so that the relationships between them are clearly understood by your readers.

Parallelism: This is one of the most useful writing devices available to the writer of better business letters. When used correctly and appropriately, it can bring order and clarity to much of your writing. Thus the second section of this lesson will show you how to apply this writing device and how to avoid some of the more common errors associated with it.

LINKS

1a

The two most commonly used links are "and" and "but." "And" is a signal that says to the reader, "Here comes another idea," while "but" says, "Here comes a contrasting idea." When used correctly, these links can help your reader understand the relationships between your ideas.

    A.   Air freight is very fast.

    B.   It is expensive.

Sentence A above expresses (an advantage/a disadvantage) of air freight.

Sentence B expresses (an advantage/a disadvantage) of air freight.

. . . .

    an advantage
    a disadvantage

1b

    A. Air freight is very fast.

    B. It is expensive.

Therefore, Sentence B expresses (an additional/a contrasting) idea.

. . . .

    a contrasting

1c

Fill in the appropriate link in the following:

    Air freight is very fast, _____ it is expensive.

. . . .

    but

1d

Fill in the appropriate link in the following:

    Air freight is very fast, _____ it is convenient.

. . . .

    and   (The second idea is merely an additional idea. Thus, "and" is the appropriate link in this case.)

2

Fill in the appropriate links in the following:

A. The convention didn't generate any new ideas, _____ we enjoyed the debate with the other delegates.

B. Our canning plant processes about sixty tons of crabs a day, _____ the cans are then shipped to our Seattle warehouse for distribution.

C. We will arrive in Chicago on Tuesday, _____ we will be staying at the Conrad Hilton.

D. We received your order for six cartons of X216 paper rolls, _____ our inventory of X216 is temporarily depleted.

. . . .

A. but   B. and   C. and   D. but

3

The three links "or," "for," and "nor" are used in the following ways:

OR is used to link alternative ideas:

We expect Recon Industries' stock to climb ten points next month, *or* the bottom will drop out of it.

FOR is used when your second idea supports the first:

I didn't expect their stock to rise so soon, *for* it was dropping when I bought it.

NOR is used to link two negative ideas:

I didn't expect their stock to rise so soon, *nor* did I buy it for that reason.

Fill in the appropriate links in the following:

A. I know she is intelligent and efficient, _____ she has worked with me for five years.

B. The tellers were not shown how to detect counterfeit currency, _____ were they told what to do with the phony bills when they did detect them.

C. You may sell your bonds _____ convert them into shares of stock on a seven-for-one basis.

· ·

A. for   B. nor   C. or

4

Match each link below with the relationship it indicates by writing the appropriate letters next to the appropriate numbers.

LINK	RELATIONSHIP
	Indicates that the next idea will be:
_____ 1. and	A. a contrasting idea
_____ 2. but	B. a supporting idea
_____ 3. or	C. an additional idea
_____ 4. for	D. another negative idea
_____ 5. nor	E. an alternative idea

· ·

1. C
2. A
3. E
4. B
5. D

5

Fill in the appropriate link in each of the following:

    A. He is an efficient _____ nervous worker.

    B. She is an efficient _____ accurate worker.

    C. She is not an efficient worker _____ is she accurate.

    D. He could be an efficient worker _____ an accurate one, but not both.

    E. He can be a very efficient worker at times, _____ I have seen him produce almost twice as many bottles as his fellow workers on a given day.

· ·

    A. but   B. and   C. nor   D. or   E. for

6

Match each set of links below with the relationship it indicates by writing the appropriate letters next to the appropriate numbers.

<u>LINK</u>

<u>RELATIONSHIP</u>

Indicates that the next idea will be:

_____ 1. { moreover / furthermore / also }

    A. a contrasting idea

_____ 2. { however / nevertheless }

    B. a result of a previous idea or follow logically from a previous idea

_____ 3. { consequently / therefore / hence / thus }

    C. an additional idea

· ·

1. C
2. A
3. B

7

Match each link on the right below with the one on left with the same meaning by writing the appropriate letters next to the appropriate numbers.

_____ 1. however   A. and

_____ 2. furthermore   B. but

_____ 3. moreover

_____ 4. nevertheless

_____ 5. also

· ·

1. B
2. A
3. A
4. B
5. A

8a

Links like "and" and "but" are usually used to connect ideas *within* sentences, while links like "moreover" and "however" are usually used to connect ideas *between* sentences. For example:

> The new product is definitely more effective than the old one, *but* it is more expensive.

> The new product is definitely more effective than the old one. It is, *however*, more expensive.

Insert the appropriate link in the following:

> The employees worked ten-hour shifts around the clock for three weeks.
>
> _____, they were not able to finish the job by the deadline date of January 10.

· ·

> However, Nevertheless

8b

Unlike links such as "and" and "but," which can be placed in only one position within a sentence, links such as "however" can be placed in several positions. However, since they are usually used to connect two sentences, they should be placed near the beginning of the second sentence.

Rewrite the second sentence above so that the link is near the beginning, but not at the beginning.

_____

_____

· ·

> They were not able, however, to finish the job by the deadline date of January 10.
>
> or
>
> They were, however, not able to finish the job by the deadline date of January 10.
>
> (This second version is a little awkward. The first answer is preferable.)

9

THEREFORE is often used to indicate that the upcoming idea follows logically from the previous idea:

> Only employees with Top Secret security clearances are allowed access to the files in Vault A. Ms. Haines has only a Secret clearance. *Therefore*, Ms. Haines is not allowed access to the files in Vault A.

CONSEQUENTLY is often used to indicate that a result is upcoming:

> The elevators were not working yesterday morning. *Consequently*, many of our office personnel were late.

Both links, however, can be used interchangeably, as synonyms. So, when you have a clear case of logical deduction use "therefore," and when you have an obvious case of cause-effect, use "consequently." In other cases, let your instincts tell you which is better.

Insert the appropriate links in the following:

> In the past six months, there have been eleven serious car accidents at the Greens
>
> Point intersection. _____, the city installed a traffic light last
>
> week.

> A meeting of the Executive Council has decided to award an extra week's vacation
>
> and a $500 bonus to all salespeople who surpass their quotas by 25% before
>
> July 16. _____, Mr. Cable will be able to take his family to Lake
>
> Mead if he sells just ten more units next week.

· ·

Consequently
Therefore

10

Fill in the appropriate links in the following:

A. We will try to deliver your shipment by June 2 as you requested, _____
    _____ we cannot guarantee delivery before June 15.

B. We will deliver your shipment of men's suits by June 2, in plenty of time for
    the opening of your store. _____, I'm happy to tell you
    that we are increasing your discount rate to 20% in honor of your new
    venture.

. . . .

A. but

    (These two ideas could also be linked as follows: "We will try to deliver your
    shipment by June 2 as you requested; however, we cannot guarantee delivery
    before June 15.")

B. Moreover, Furthermore, Also

11

Fill in the appropriate links in the following:

A. This training program has been developed in consultation with experienced
    bankers _____ has been thoroughly tested on bank employees.

B. This training program has been developed in consultation with experienced
    bankers. _____ , it has been thoroughly tested on bank employees.

C. The weather bureau now predicts a late spring next year; _____ ,
    we can expect completion of the Rochester plant to be delayed at least a
    month.

D. I am increasingly alarmed by the drop-off in production at the Mercer Island
    factory. _____, I have learned through confidential sources that
    the union plans to strike us within two weeks.

E. Over the years, we have maintained a profit-sharing plan for those managers who show exceptional merit. Our competition, _____, has not been able to lure our best people away from us.

F. This client usually pays for a purchase with cash _____ by personal check.

G. I know the problems of that company as well as anybody, _____ I have been on its Board of Directors for the last ten years.

. . . .

A. and
B. Furthermore, Moreover, Also
C. Consequently, Therefore
D. Furthermore, Moreover, Also
E. consequently, therefore
F. or
G. for

12

Fill in the appropriate links in the following:

In order to coincide with the publication date, advertising promotion for your new cookbook will begin on August 10. _____, sales should be brisk until well into September, when they will probably fall off a bit. _____, we do expect heavy sales during the Christmas season and will probably go into a second printing early next year. In fact, we may have to do this earlier if reviews are exceptionally good _____ if one of the book clubs decides to pick it up.

. . . .

Consequently, Therefore
However
or

13

Below is a paragraph in which necessary links have been omitted. Read it over first and then improve it by inserting appropriate links. You may edit and combine the sentences.

The paintings you asked for were crated. We shipped them via air-freight last Tuesday. We were not able to find your Aztec pottery in our Bleeker Street warehouse. A search of the files did not disclose any record of it either. We have sent a letter of inquiry in your behalf to Mason Brothers Storage, Inc., since they may have kept the pottery after the World's Fair exhibition.

. . . .

The paintings you asked for were crated. ~~We~~ shipped ~~them~~ via air-freight last

[inserted: **and**]

Tuesday. ~~We~~ were not able to find your Aztec pottery in our Bleeker Street

[inserted: **However, we**]

warehouse. ~~A~~ search of the files ~~did not~~ disclose any record of it ~~either. We~~

[inserted: **, nor did a** ... **Consequently, we**]

have sent a letter of inquiry in your behalf to Mason Brothers Storage, Inc., since they may have kept the pottery after the World's Fair exhibition.

(Notice how smoothly the above paragraph flows after the links have been inserted.)

PARALLELISM

14

Parallelism is a writing device which allows you to say to your reader, "Here are some ideas which have something in common and which I have arranged side by side in the same grammatical form." Parallelism allows you to bring symmetry and order to your writing.

All of the words, except one, in each of the groups below have something in common. Circle the discordant word in each group.

think	inventory	swiftly
consider	stock	slowly
ponder	merchandise	quickly
talk	invoice	rapidly

. . . .

think	inventory	swiftly
consider	stock	(slowly)
ponder	merchandise	quickly
(talk)	(invoice)	rapidly

15

In each of the following groups of words, one word doesn't have the same grammatical form as the others. Circle it.

thinking	inventory	swiftly
considered	stock	quick
pondered	merchandised	rapidly

. . . .

(thinking)	inventory	swiftly
considered	stock	(quick)
pondered	(merchandised)	rapidly

16a

Ideas that have something in common are said to be parallel, as are words and groups of words that have the same grammatical form. Thus when you express parallel ideas in parallel grammatical forms, you are using the device of parallelism.

Below are two versions of the same thought. In which one are parallel ideas expressed in parallel forms? _____

    A. The mail room receives incoming mail, which is then sorted, and an employee delivers it.

    B. The mail room receives, sorts, and delivers all incoming mail.

. . . .

    B

16b

Circle the parallel words in sentence B above.

. . . .

    B. The mail room (receives,) (sorts,) and (delivers) all incoming mail.

17a

    Our company has a reputation for *high-quality work*, for *progressive management*, and for *being reliable.*

Do the above three italicized word groups express parallel ideas? _____

. . . .

    yes

17b

Are they expressed in parallel grammatical forms? _____

. . . .

    no

17c

Circle the phrase that is not parallel.

. . . .

Our company has a reputation for *high-quality work*, for *progressive management*, and for (being reliable.)

17d

Make this item parallel with the others by completing the following:

Our company has a reputation for high-quality work, for progressive management, and for _____.

. . . .

reliability

18a

In which of the following sentences are parallel ideas expressed in parallel forms?

A. We are not responsible for lost or stolen articles or any items that have been misplaced.

B. If we receive your order before June 10, we can promise delivery by the end of the month.

C. If you will prepare the letter, our staff will address, stuff, and mail the envelopes.

. . . .

C

18b

Rewrite sentence A above so that it expresses its parallel ideas in parallel grammatical forms.

_____

_____

_____

. . . .

We are not responsible for lost, stolen, or misplaced articles (items).

19

Parallel ideas may be expressed in:

1. parallel single words, or

2. parallel phrases, or

3. parallel clauses, or

4. parallel independent clauses.

Each of the following sentences contains one of the above parallel constructions. Write the number of each grammatical form after the sentence that exemplifies it.

A. We will consider locating in an office building, in an apartment house, or in a commercial loft. _____

B. This stock tends to rise in the summer, and it tends to decline in the winter.

_____

C. The speech was monotonous, wordy, and vague. _____

D. We are looking for applicants who are intelligent and who are willing to work hard. _____

. . . .

A. 2   B. 4   C. 1   D. 3

20a

After the clerk told us where to go, he then instructed us on what to do and also how to do it.

Circle the three parallel ideas in the sentence above.

· ·

After the clerk told us (where to go,) he then instructed us on (what to do) and also (how to do it.)

20b

Now rewrite the sentence:

The clerk told us _____, _____, and

_____.

· ·

The clerk told us *where to go, what to do*, and *how to do it.*

21

After the lathes are crated at the factory, we then ship them from our warehouse.

Rewrite the above sentence so that it expresses its parallel ideas in parallel grammatical forms.

_____

_____

· ·

We crate the lathes at the factory and ship them from our warehouse.   (active)

or

The lathes are crated at the factory and shipped from our warehouse.   (passive)

22

This computer is fast, accurate, and can be programmed easily.

Rewrite the above sentence so that it expresses its parallel ideas in parallel grammatical forms.

_____

_____

_____

. . . .

This computer is fast, accurate, and easy to program.

or

This computer is fast, accurate, and easily programmed.

23a

. . . either . . . or . . .
. . . neither . . . nor . . .
. . . not only . . . but also . . .

These sets of words, called "correlatives," are used to join parallel ideas. They should always be followed by grammatical forms that are identical. For example:

Mrs. Hayes will allow Jack either *to go* to the San Francisco Conference or *to meet* Mr. Townes at our office, but not both.

Note that the grammatical constructions immediately following "either" and "or" are identical, as they should be.

Now look at the following:

We hoped *not only* to obtain realistic production estimates from the new management group *but also* a summary of raw-material needs was aimed at.

Are the grammatical forms following each of the correlatives identical? _____

. . . .

no

23b

Rewrite the above sentence so that the forms following the two correlatives are parallel.

_____

_____

_____
. . . .

We hoped not only *to obtain* realistic production estimates from the new management group but also *to summarize* raw material needs.

24

Mr. Yasinski was neither willing to learn nor did he have the ability to accept criticism.

Rewrite the above sentence so that the grammatical forms following "neither" and "nor" are parallel.

_____

_____
. . . .

Mr. Yasinski was neither *willing* to learn nor *able* to accept criticism.

or

Mr. Yasinski was willing neither *to learn* nor *to accept* criticism.

(Note that these two versions have slightly different meanings.)

25a

Which of the following sentences exemplify the correct use of parallelism? _____

A. In September, the inventory of Allied Flour Mills increases as it purchases the summer wheat harvest; and in November, its inventory decreases as it sells flour to its customers.

B. The stock market remained steady on Wednesday, rose slightly on Thursday, and was observed to drop sharply on Friday.

C. Our employment office will be open Tuesday to accept applications and for interviews.

D. The newly hired salespeople are trained, given sample cases, assigned territories, and then we let them out on their own.

E. Elaine not only attended the sales meeting but delivered a pep talk.

. . . .

A and E

25b

Cross out the parts of sentences B, C, and D that need reworking and insert your revisions.

. . . .

B. The stock market remained steady on Wednesday, rose slightly on Thursday,

    and ~~was observed to drop~~ sharply on Friday.
          dropped
          ∧

C. Our employment office will be open Tuesday to accept applications and

    ~~for~~ interviews.
     ∧
    to conduct, hold, give, etc.

    or

    Our employment office will be open Tuesday ~~to accept~~ applications and
                                                    for
                                                    ∧
    for interviews.

D. The newly hired salespeople are trained, given sample cases, assigned terri-
    tories, and then ~~we~~ let ~~them~~ out on their own.

26

The following paragraph can be improved by a more intelligent application of the
principle of parallelism. Write in your revisions so that parallel ideas are expressed in
parallel forms.

I received your proposal for the development of better sales forecasting methods,
and it has been forwarded by me to our Executive Board for their consideration.
With it, I included not only my own evaluation of your general plan but I gave my
opinion as to the accuracy of your cost estimates. Needless to say, I enthusi-
astically endorsed both parts as being realistic and they are carefully thought out.

. . . .

I received your proposal for the development of better sales forecasting methods

      forwarded it
and ~~it has been forwarded by me~~ to our Executive Board for their consideration.
         ^
With it, I included not only my own evaluation of your general plan but ~~I gave~~ my
opinion as to the accuracy of your cost estimates. Needless to say, I enthusi-
astically endorsed both parts as being realistic and ~~they are~~ carefully thought out.

Another way to revise the second sentence is as follows:

                    not only
With it, I included ~~not only~~ my own evaluation of your general plan of operation
                                  ^

    of
but ~~I gave my opinion as to~~ the accuracy of your cost estimates.
   ^

This is the end of Lesson 3. Now turn to page 175 and take the Quiz for Lesson 3.

LESSON 4 BEING NATURAL, COURTEOUS, AND PERSONAL

This lesson will help you achieve a natural, courteous, and personal style in your business letters. For it is just as important that your letters have these qualities as it is that they be clear and concise. Think for a moment about the way people speak to and interact with each other in business. Have you noticed that the ones who are most successful and effective usually are able to express themselves in a simple, unaffected manner? They are able, somehow, to give the impression that they are courteous and considerate—that they *care* about the people around them—while at the same time concentrating on the business at hand. However, it is the stuffed shirts and the loud-mouths who are usually the butt of office jokes.

Isn't it logical to conclude that the style which most succeeds in the office is also the style that can best work in business letters? This may seem obvious, but unfortunately, some of the most fluent and effective business people become cold, pompous jargon-eers when they write letters. They feel that they have to fit their natural conversational mode of expression into a rigid mold called "the business writing style." For example, below is a letter written by an insurance adjuster to a customer who has had a car accident and has applied for damage benefits.

July 20

Dear Mrs. Harding:

Please be advised that the letter under date of June 6 would have been answered at a prior date to the present, if it had not been the case that it was addressed to the wrong department. Hereinafter, kindly address all correspondence in reference to your claim for damage benefits to the Automobile Liability Claims Division.

You claim that three individuals were witness to the alleged accident. However, this office cannot undertake consideration of the claim until such time as the names and addresses of these individuals are furnished us.

Sincerely,

Everett Stillwell

This letter would probably inspire the reader with all the kindly instincts of a chicken hawk. It is pompous, rude, and cold primarily because of four basic faults. First, it contains archaic expressions such as "under date" and "hereinafter." This kind of wording was popular in business at the turn of the century, but since most firms do not want to appear old-fashioned, you would do well to eliminate all archaic expressions from your letters.

Second, the above letter contains many examples of inflated writing. This fault occurs because the writer chooses to use long, complex words when short, simple ones would serve just as well. Note that the above writer has used expressions such as "a prior date" and "with reference to" when "sooner" and "about" would serve better.

This tendency to use inflated words stems from a slightly dishonest impulse that most letter writers experience when they find that they have something fairly simple and ordinary to say. So, to avoid the implication that *they* are simple and ordinary, they dress their words up to suggest a formality that is not strictly truthful. It is such impulses, for example, that lead them to write, "A thorough investigation was made as to the subject's whereabouts," instead of "I looked up his address in the telephone book."

The "Armed Forces Management" magazine touched on the subject of inflated writing in the following way:

INSTANT EXPERTISE*

A new aid for preparing speeches, briefings, etc. is circulating in the Defense Department. The "Buzzphrase Generator" gives instant expertise on matters pertaining to defense. Here it is:

COLUMN 1	COLUMN 2	COLUMN 3
0 integrated	0 management	0 options
1 total	1 organizational	1 flexibility
2 systematized	2 monitored	2 capability
3 parallel	3 reciprocal	3 mobility
4 functional	4 digital	4 programming
5 responsive	5 logistical	5 concept
6 optimal	6 transitional	6 time-phase
7 synchronized	7 incremental	7 projection
8 compatible	8 third-generation	8 hardware
9 balanced	9 policy	9 contingency

The procedure is simple. Think of any three-digit number. Select the corresponding buzzword from each column. Put them together and WHAM! POW! ZAP! You sound just like you know what you're talking about.

For instance, take the number 257. You get "systematized logistical projection." Would you prefer 349 (parallel digital contingency) or 935 (balanced reciprocal concept)? You don't know what it means, but don't worry, neither do "they." The important result is that the user now has the perfect aid for preparing any communication on the subject of national defense.

A third fault of the above letter is that it has too many negative thoughts and words. Note that the first sentence makes it abundantly clear to the reader that she has made a grievous error by sending her letter to the "wrong department." Certainly the reader, who happens to be a customer of the company, made a mistake. But why rub it in?

---

*Reprinted from *Armed Forces Management*.

The second sentence adds further offense by summarily ordering this customer to use the right address from here on. In the third sentence, the words "claim" and "alleged" imply that the reader may be lying about the witnesses and even about the accident itself. And the last sentence is again full of negative words.

The fourth fault is that the letter is too impersonal. Note that the writer avoids mention of himself or his firm most of the time by using the passive voice, and when he does refer to his firm, he calls it "this office."

This lesson will help you avoid these faults by encouraging you to write in a simple conversational style, to be courteous and positive, and to be personal by using a liberal sprinkling of words such as "I," "you," and "we." Thus we hope you will write letters, not like the one above, but like the one below.

> Dear Mrs. Harding:
>
> I would have answered your letter of June 6 sooner, but it has just been forwarded to me from our Actuarial Department. I assure you that you will receive much more efficient service from us if you will address all future letters concerning your claim for automobile damage benefits to me, care of the Automobile Liability Claims Division.
>
> In your letter, you said that three people witnessed the accident. May I have the names and addresses of these witnesses? As soon as I receive them, we will be happy to give prompt consideration to your claim.
>
> Sincerely,
>
> Everett Stillwell

INFLATED WORDS

1

Below are a list of inflated phrases and a list of simple ones that mean exactly the same thing. Match them by writing the appropriate letter next to the appropriate number.

INFLATED		SIMPLE	
_____ 1.	we deem it advisable	A.	I am sorry that
_____ 2.	with reference to	B.	we suggest
_____ 3.	I regret to inform you that	C.	as you asked
_____ 4.	as requested by you	D.	about

· ·

    1. B
    2. D
    3. A
    4. C

2a

Subsequent to your arrival, we will meet to discuss the program in Conference Room A.

Cross out the inflated phrase in the above sentence.

· ·

~~Subsequent to your arrival~~, we will meet to discuss the program in Conference Room A.

2b

Now write a deflated version of this phrase over the crossed-out portion in our answer above.

· ·

    After you arrive
~~Subsequent to your arrival~~, we will meet to discuss the program in Conference
         ^
Room A.

3

Cross out the inflated phrase in the following sentence and write in a simpler version.

I will call you prior to your departure.

. . . .

         before you leave
I will call you ~~prior to your departure~~.

4

Cross out the inflated words in each of the following sentences and write in simpler versions.

A. I regret to inform you that your contest entry arrived after the closing date.

B. I am writing with reference to your order #SA6201 which we sent out subsequent to your cancellation order.

C. It is deemed advisable that all production of the pump be stopped until you discover the source of the leaks.

D. We have sent your order by rail as requested by you.

. . . .

       I am sorry but
A. ~~I regret to inform you that~~ your contest entry arrived after the closing date.
         ^

           about
B. I am writing ~~with reference to~~ your order #SA6201 which we sent out
               ^

  after
~~subsequent to~~ your cancellation order.

  We, I suggest, think
C. ~~It is deemed advisable~~ that all production of X692 be stopped until you dis-
         ^

cover the source of the leak.

                  you asked
D. We have sent your order by rail as ~~requested by you~~.
                           ^

5

The following sentence is inflated. Rewrite it.

I consider it advisable that you initiate a chemical analyzation of the foreign material at once.

. . . .

I suggest that you chemically analyze the foreign material at once.

6

Deflate the following letter by crossing out any inflated language and writing your revision over it. You may want to revise whole sentences since several are very wordy— another characteristic of inflated writing.

CENTROFLUX, INC.
"Your Neighborhood Appliance Center"
11 Greenwood Avenue

May 21,

Mr. T.E. Waterman
15 Emery Place

Dear Mr. Waterman:

It is regrettable to have to inform you that we cannot replace your washing machine as requested by you in your letter of May 19, since the breakdown occurred subsequent to the expiration of the guaranty. However, I have been informed that in the event that your washer undergoes repair at one of our service centers, the cost that will be incurred by you will be only for the labor of those individuals involved in such labor.

. . . .

I am sorry but
~~It is regrettable to have to inform you that~~ we cannot replace your washing
∧
you asked
machine as ~~requested by you~~ in your letter of May 19, since the breakdown
∧
after the guaranty expired.   if
occurred ~~subsequent to the expiration of the guaranty~~. However, ~~I have been in-~~
∧   ∧
is repaired
~~formed that in the event that~~ your washer ~~undergoes repair~~ at one of our service
∧
to
centers, the cost ~~that will be incurred by~~ you will be only for ~~the~~ labor ~~of those~~
∧

~~individuals involved in such labor~~.

The letter should now read something like this:

Dear Mr. Waterman:

I am sorry but we cannot replace your washing machine as you asked in your letter of May 19, since the breakdown occurred after the guaranty expired. However, if your washer is repaired at one of our service centers, the cost to you will be for labor only.

ARCHAIC EXPRESSIONS

7a

Archaic expressions, like inflated language, can hamper the tone of your letters. For example:

Pursuant to our agreement, I am enclosing a sight draft for $12,000.

Circle the archaic expression in the above sentence.

. . . .

(Pursuant to our agreement,) I am enclosing a sight draft for $12,000.

7b

A more natural substitution for this archaic phrase is "As we agreed." Another pet phrase of the ancients is "as per." Cross out this archaic expression in the following sentence and write in your revision.

As per our discussion, I have arranged a meeting with the Pedicone group for next

Tuesday.

· ·

As we discussed, agreed,

~~As per our discussion~~, I have arranged a meeting with the Pedicone group for next
       ∧

Tuesday.

7c

As per your letter of April 9, we are enclosing two copies of our application form.

"As per" in the above sentence probably means "as you requested." What does it mean in the following?

_____

As per your suggestion in your letter of May 14, I think we should by all means

give a raise to the top three salespersons of each division.

· ·

As you suggested

8

Write a simple substitute over each of the archaic phrases crossed out below.

    A. ~~Enclosed herewith find~~ six copies of the cost-accounting report for distribu-
        tion to your managers.

    B. I have ~~duly noted~~ your letter of January 9, and agree wholeheartedly with
        your conclusions.

· ·

    A. Here are, Enclosed are

    B. read

9

Cross out the archaic phrases in the following paragraph and write your corrections over them.

> As per your request letter of March 10, we will deliver a dictaphone to your main office on Monday. And pursuant to our arrangement, you will herewith find an installment-loan contract, which you should duly note and then affix your signature.

. . . .

> As you requested in
> ~~As per~~ your ~~request~~ letter of March 10, we will deliver a dictaphone to your main
>   ∧
>
>   as we arranged,   here is, I am enclosing, etc.
> office on Monday. And ~~pursuant to our arrangement, you will herewith find~~
>   ∧   ∧
>
>   read   sign.
> an installment-loan contract, which you should ~~duly note~~ and then ~~affix your~~
>   ∧   ∧
> ~~signature.~~

This paragraph should now read something like this:

> As you requested in your letter of March 10, we will deliver a dictaphone to your main office on Monday. And as we arranged, here is an installment-loan contract, which you should read and then sign.

POSITIVE AND NEGATIVE WORDS

10

Words not only have a dictionary meaning but an emotional meaning. Thus, when most of us read or hear words like "truth," "efficiency," "thank you," "improve," or "beauty," we tend to react pleasantly or positively. And when we are exposed to words like "arrogant," "you cannot," "pest," or "childish," our reactions usually are unpleasant or negative. However, some words, such as "fork," "mercantile," "policy," "smooth," or "travel," do not have much emotional meaning and thus they usually have a neutral effect on most of us.

Since a large majority of business letters are written to convey neutral facts and ideas, most of your letters will have a high proportion of neutral words. But you should realize that even the most ordinary or routine letter carries certain emotional over-tones, either positive or negative. This ingredient becomes of primary importance when you are writing letters which convey thoughts and facts that can affect the reader's emotions. For example, a letter turning down an application for credit or employment has a high potential for doing great damage to the reader's feelings. In such letters, it is extremely important that the words you use are as neutral or positive as you can make them.

Below are three groups of words which more or less have the same dictionary meaning. In each group is a positive word, a negative word, and a neutral word. Put a plus (+) next to the positive words, a minus (−) next to the negative ones, and a zero (0) next to the neutral ones.

limousine	_____	cautious	_____	Hitler	_____
automobile	_____	prudent	_____	leader	_____
pile of junk	_____	cowardly	_____	Abraham Lincoln	_____

· ·

limousine	+	cautious	0	Hitler	−
automobile	0	prudent	+	leader	0
pile of junk	−	cowardly	−	Abraham Lincoln	+

11

Do the same thing for the following list of words:

punctual	_____	worry	_____
book	_____	unfair	_____
pen	_____	loyalty	_____
genuine	_____	tardy	_____
You must go to . . .	_____	Please send us . . .	_____
It is impossible to . . .	_____	I appreciate . . .	_____
because	_____	incorrect	_____

. . . .

punctual	+	worry	−
book	0	unfair	−
pen	0	loyalty	+
genuine	+	tardy	−
You must go to . . .	−	Please send us . . .	+
It is impossible to . . .	−	I appreciate . . .	+
because	0	incorrect	−

12a

I have found out that you are delinquent for three installment-loan payments. Circle the negative word or words that make this unnecessarily offensive.

. . . .

I (have found out) that you are (delinquent) for three installment-loan payments.

12b

I have found out that you are delinquent for three installment-loan payments.

Replace the negative words in our answer above with positive or neutral words if possible or with less negative words at least.

. . . .

    notice, see, etc.   late in making, overdue on, behind on, etc.

I (have found out) that you are (delinquent) ~~for~~ three installment-loan payments.

13

No one enjoys being ordered about, whereas most of us react favorably to being asked.

Which of the following two sentences is most likely to get a favorable response?

    A.   Payment of this invoice must reach our office by October 31.

    B.   May we have your payment by October 31?

. . . .

    B

14

Change the following sentence to a more courteous request:

    A prompt reply would be appreciated.

. . . .

    May we hear from you soon?

    or

    Please reply as soon as possible.

15

Many times we emphasize the negative side of things rather than the positive. For instance:

Our office does not open until 9:45 a.m.

Doesn't the following say the same thing, but more positively?

Our office opens at 9:45 a.m.

Change the following sentence to emphasize the positive:

Our office is closed after 5:15 p.m.

. . . .

                open until
Our office is ~~closed after~~ 5:15 p.m.
                ∧

16

We cannot deliver your shipment before next week.

Why tell the reader what you cannot do when you can just as easily tell him what you can do? Why not say:

We will be happy to deliver your shipment next week at the latest.

Revise the following sentence so that it tells the reader what *can* be done:

Because our next board meeting is not scheduled until January 13, we will not be

able to consider your proposal until then.

_____

_____

_____
. . . .

We will be glad to consider your proposal at our next board meeting on January 13.

17

Sometimes, of course, the thought you are trying to express is necessarily negative—as, for instance, when you must refuse a request. However, you can soften the negative tone by eliminating any arrogant or condescending overtones.

> As you would know if you read our guaranty carefully, we do not repair damage caused by customer negligence.

Your reader may be at fault, but why not say,

> I would like to grant your request, but our guaranty only covers the cost of replacing defective parts.

Revise the offensiveness out of the following sentence:

> Your application for this job has been denied since we specifically stated at the time you applied that we would only consider college graduates.

_____

_____

_____
. . . .

> Because we are specifically looking for a college graduate, I am sorry we cannot consider your application for this job.

18

We are returning your loan application because you forgot to sign it. Therefore, we cannot process this form until you sign it in the space in the lower left-hand corner, which is clearly marked for this purpose, and return it promptly.

Revise this to make it more courteous and positive. You may cut out some parts of it.

_____

_____

_____

_____

. . . .

We will be glad to process your loan application as soon as you sign it in the lower left-hand corner and return it to us.

_____

19

The following letter is designed to antagonize the reader. Rewrite it.

CENTRAL TELEPHONE COMPANY
118 Liberty Street

December 15

Miss Georgia Reilly
11 Maiden Lane

Dear Miss Reilly:

This office has no record of any check received for payment of your October telephone bill as you claim. Therefore, unless you can furnish proof that you actually paid this bill, we will be forced to consider terminating you service.

_____

_____

_____

_____

_____

. . . .

Dear Miss Reilly:

We cannot find any record of payment of your October telephone bill. Could you therefore send us a copy of your canceled check so that we can correct our files?

20

Rewrite the following letter so that it is both positive and friendly:

JASON CHARTER TOURS, INC.
135 West 10th Street

January 10

Mr. Howard Bjorklund
110 Norris Avenue

Dear Mr. Bjorklund:

We have no seats on our Hawaii Charter Tour flight for February 1, nor will we have any until March 1. Also, our London Charter Tour flights are sold out until March 1.

A deposit of $150 per person must accompany each reservation. Promptness is recommended.

_____

_____

_____

_____

_____

_____

. . . .

Dear Mr. Bjorklund:

We would like to accept your reservation on our Hawaii Charter Tour flight for February 1, but seats for both our Hawaii and London Charter Tours are available only on March 1 and after.

If you will send us a check right away for a deposit of $150 per person, we will be happy to accept your reservation on a later flight.

THE PERSONAL TOUCH

21a

Many business writers must write letters that deal with the same problems over and over. Naturally, they tend to forget that their readers are individuals and that each one's problem is a little different from the next. However, writers of more effective business letters do not forget. They make a conscious effort to think of each reader as a person. Even a form letter that is sent to thousands of people can have the personal touch.

Which of the following paragraphs from a form letter is more personal? _____

    A. Our new computer seems to have run amuck this week and added three extra 000's to each of our checks. If you have been one of the astonished recipients of such a check, please return it to us and we will send you one for the correct amount at once.

    B. A flaw in the electronic computer has resulted in the addition of an extra three zeros to all checks issued this week. If such a check has been received, it would be much appreciated if it were returned at once and a replacement with the correct amount will be issued.

. . . .

    A

21b

The first paragraph is more personal because it has several "you's" and "we's."

How many "you's" and "we's" are in the second? _____

. . . .

    none

22

One of the best ways to make your letters personal is to sprinkle them liberally with "I," "you," and "we." Use "I" when you are speaking for yourself. Use "we" when you are speaking for a group within your organization or for the organization itself. Don't use "we" in such expressions as "we are sorry that you did not receive courteous service at our candy counter," since "we" in this case refers to the firm, and it is somewhat insincere to imply that the firm is "sorry." Instead, use "I" in such cases.

Rewrite the following sentence so that it is more personal:

It is assured that the deadline will be met by this firm.

_____

_____

. . . .

I assure you that we will meet the deadline.

or

You can be sure that we will meet the deadline.

23

It is felt that your cost estimates should be reviewed by this writer before they are presented to Ms. Erhardt.

Rewrite the above so it is more personal.

_____

_____

. . . .

I feel (think) that I should review your cost estimates before you present them to Ms. Erhardt.

or

I feel (think) that I should review your cost estimates before Ms. Erhardt sees them.

24

Write in the appropriate pronoun in each of the following:

A. The editors and I have read your manuscript and _____ like it.

B. _____ require an average of ten tons of rolled steel per month.

C. _____ will call you next week regarding my decision.

D. _____ am/are sorry you have had bad luck with our blender.

E. Due to the recent strikes, _____ have been running late on deliveries this month.

. . . .

A. we   B. we   C. I   D. I am   E. we

25

Cross out any pronouns that are incorrect or impersonal and write your revisions over them.

We are glad to hear from anyone who tried our coffee and liked it. True, the price is a little higher than that of other blends—but then, the blend this firm uses is of higher quality and people usually find that they can use a smaller amount of our coffee to make more cups.

. . . .

I am   that you   our
We are glad to hear from anyone who tried our coffee and liked it. True, the price
  ∧   ∧   ∧

                                           our
is a little higher than that of other blends—but then, the blend this firm uses is of

              you will   you
higher quality and people usually find that they can use a smaller amount of our
               ∧   ∧

coffee to make more cups.

26

Sometimes business writers, in their efforts to insert "I," "you," and "we," will use too much "I" and "we." In other words, they talk too much about themselves and their organizations. However, readers are primarily interested in themselves and like to see a lot of "you's."

> I'm always glad to receive a letter from one of our customers who is satisfied with
>
> our Jet Beam Flashlight.

The reader probably is not interested in how the writer feels. Rewrite this by putting the emphasis on "you."

_____

_____

_____

. . . .

> Thank you for your letter indicating your satisfaction with your Jet Beam Flashlight.
>
> or
>
> I'm glad to hear that you are satisfied with your Jet Beam Flashlight.

27

Cross out the words in the following sentence that make it too self-centered and insert your revisions over them.

> I'm sorry to learn that anyone is dissatisfied with our new Fluff-Dry Hairdryer.

. . . .

>   you are   your
>
> I'm sorry to learn that ~~anyone is~~ dissatisfied with ~~our~~ new Fluff-Dry Hairdryer.

28

> I was glad to hear of your appointment to Chief of the Paris Bureau.

Why emphasize how your reader's appointment made you feel? Wouldn't it be more to the point to simply congratulate him?

> Congratulations on
> ~~I was glad to hear of~~ your appointment to Chief of the Paris Bureau.
>   ∧

Now do the same for the following sentence:

> I'm glad to hear of your decision to stay on and help us out with the Stone-Paine project.

. . . .

> Thanks for deciding
> ~~I'm glad to hear of your decision~~ to stay on and help us out with the Stone-Paine
>   ∧
> project.

29

> We offer two medical plans: one for individuals only and one that can include members of their immediate family.

The above sentence not only is addressed to a statistic but it also emphasizes what you do rather than what the reader can do. Rewrite it.

_____

_____

_____
. . . .

> You can take out a medical plan for yourself only or one that can include your immediate family.

REVIEW

30

In this lesson you have learned about deflating inflated language, updating archaic expressions, eliminating negative overtones, and making your letters personal.

Each of the following sentences contains one or more faults. Cross them out and write your corrections over them.

A. As per your order for twenty bales of cotton, we cannot deliver them before August 6.

B. It is deemed advisable by those in this office that your short-term debt should be decreased by the issuance of debentures in the amount of $1,000,000.

C. Orders for additional fur pieces must reach this office prior to June 10.

D. I was glad to find your report as excellent as I expected it to be.

E. As requested in your letter of November 25, an application for credit is herewith enclosed.

. . . .

A. <u>Regarding, As for</u> your order for twenty bales of cotton, we cannot deliver them <u>before</u>   <u>after</u>
August 6.

or

We can deliver your order for twenty bales of cotton after August 6.

B. <u>It is deemed advisable by those in this office</u> that your short-term debt <u>should</u>
We think, We feel   you should decrease
<u>be decreased</u> by <u>the issuance of</u> debentures <u>in the amount of</u> $1,000,000.
issuing   for, worth

C. Orders for additional fur pieces <u>must reach this office prior to</u> June 10.
Please send your, May we have your   before

or

If you want additional fur pieces, please send your orders before June 10.

D. <u>I was glad to find your report as</u> excellent <u>as I expected it to be.</u>
Congratulations on your   report

you asked   here is, I am enclosing

E. As ~~requested~~ in your letter of November 25, an application for credit ~~is here-~~
          ^   ^
~~with enclosed.~~

31

Revise the following letter so that it is natural, courteous, and personal.

CASE PHARMACEUTICALS, INC.

118 South Street

March 12

Ms. Rose Koosis
Proprietor
Church Hill Drug Store
11 Main Street

Dear Ms. Koosis:

We have at hand your letter under date of March 9 and have duly noted the suggestion that we initiate extensive testing of our sedative, KLORSEL, because you claim it has painful side effects. However, let me hasten to make assurances that prior to any drug being released on the market, this firm submits it to a rigorous testing procedure, using both laboratory animals and selected groups of volunteers.

The opinion therefore is held by our research and testing staff that your so-called "deleterious side effects" are due to causes other than KLORSEL. Substantial evidence to the contrary is required before we could take such a suggestion into serious consideration.

_____

_____

_____

_____

_____

_____

_____

_____

_____

_____

_____

_____

_____

_____

_____

_____

_____

_____

_____

. . . .

Dear Ms. Koosis:

I have carefully read your letter of March 9, suggesting that we start extensive testing of our sedative, KLORSEL, because of the side effects. However, let me assure you that before we release any of our products on the market, we test them rigorously on both laboratory animals and selected groups of volunteers.

Could it possibly be, Ms. Koosis, that the side effects you describe are due to a cause other than KLORSEL? If you will send us your evidence that KLORSEL is the cause, we will certainly give it serious consideration.

This is the end of Lesson 4. Now turn to page 177 and take the Quiz for Lesson 4.

The starting sentence of a business letter is one of the most important parts because it makes the first impression on the reader—for good or ill. For this reason, we spend the first half of this lesson teaching some of the better ways to start a business letter.

The second half covers some of the more effective ways of closing a business letter. Because the finish is usually the most memorable part of the letter, it offers the writer a unique opportunity to emphasize the main point or make a request.

THE START

1a

The first thing your reader wants to know upon opening your letter is, "What is the letter about?" Nothing is more irritating for the reader than to wade through half the letter to find out why someone is writing. Consider the following:

REGENT MANUFACTURING, INC.
173 Creighton Avenue

June 13

Mr. Ralph Anderson
Anderson Placement Service, Inc.
148 Market Street

Dear Mr. Anderson:

A recent company-wide evaluation of our employees has led us to take a new look at our personnel policies. Thus, for the first time, we are searching for middle-management talent outside the company and would appreciate your referring to us any applicants you feel would meet our qualifications. We prefer college graduates but will also consider those with five or more years experience in administrating assembly-line production.

Suppose you have just received the above letter. Does the opening sentence give you a good idea of what the letter is about? _____

. . . .

no

1b

Underline the sentence that does.

. . . .

A recent company-wide evaluation of our employees has led us to take a new look at our personnel policies.

<u>Thus, for the first time, we are searching for middle-management talent outside the company and would appreciate your referring to us any applicants you feel would meet our qualifications.</u>

We prefer college graduates but will also consider those with five or more years experience in administrating assembly-line production.

1c

Using our answer above, rearrange the sentences by numbering them in the order in which they should appear.

. . . .

  2   A recent company-wide evaluation . . .

  1   Thus, for the first time, we . . .

  3   We prefer college graduates but . . .

(These sentences, of course, would have to be reworded for continuity if they were to be used in an actual letter.)

2

Business letters are written for many purposes: to answer inquiries, to request information, to ask the reader to do something, to decline requests, to sell something, etc. Your opening sentence does not always have to make the purpose of your letter totally explicit, but it should always give a good idea of what you are writing about.

From which of the following sentences can the reader easily learn what the letter is about? _____

A. We received your letter of March 16.

B. As you requested in your letter of March 16, we are enclosing a copy of our booklet *Plan Ahead for Retirement.*

C. This booklet shows various ways in which you can ensure a comfortable retirement after only fifteen years.

. . . .

B

3

Sometimes, you may want to give away the whole purpose of your letter in the first sentence. For example, on the left below is a list of starting sentences which do this. Match the purposes with the sentences by writing the appropriate letters next to the appropriate numbers.

OPENING SENTENCES

PURPOSES

_____ 1. If you will fill in your name and address on the enclosed postcard, our representative will be glad to visit you at your convenience to explain our New Deal Life Insurance Plan and to give you a handsome cowhide address book—free of charge.

A. to request action

_____ 2. Because your one hundred shares of Cetron Electric, Inc., have declined thirty points in the last week, we will need an additional $25,000 to increase your margin.

B. to give information

_____ 3. I understand that you are offering charter airline service and would like to know more about it.

C. to sell something

_____ 4. Your order #5906V for six hundred bushels of spring wheat has been put aboard the SS President Polk for delivery in early June.

D. to request information

. . . .

1. C
2. A
3. D
4. B

4

Below are five opening sentences. Which of them tells the reader what the letter is about? _____

    A. I received your letter of January 19.

    B. If you will fill out the enclosed questionnaire and return it to us, we will send you a free sample of our new cleanser, GLO-BRITE.

    C. At our sales meeting last week we discussed the possibility of a separate edition for younger readers.

    D. We are planning to institute a voluntary retirement plan for our professional staff.

    E. We no longer manufacture X62 and have therefore replaced your order for twenty gross of X62 with twenty gross of X63.

. . . .

    B and E

    (The reader's response to openings such as C and D is likely to be, "So what?")

5

Following are five sentences contained in a letter to a building contractor. Which should come first? _____

    A. Due to expanded business, we need more space for our office staff and records.

    B. We would like to give the contract to a local company if possible.

    C. The building will contain twenty-six office suites for rental and five ground-floor shops.

    D. We are planning to construct a building on North Street and would like to receive your bid.

    E. Bids should be received before March 16 to give us time to reach a decision by May 1.

. . . .

    D

6a

Your reader wants to know right away not only, "What is this letter about?" but, "What's in it for me?" Thus you should try to also include in your starting sentence the idea that will be of most interest to the reader—whenever possible. Look at the following:

> Fortunately, we have found a buyer for your house at an excellent price. She will be away on business for two weeks, but when she returns, she has promised to effect a closing immediately. That means you will be receiving a check for about $68,000 in about three weeks. Congratulations!

Does the starting sentence above tell the reader what the letter is about? _____

. . . .

yes

6b

Does it include the idea of paramount interest to the reader? _____

. . . .

no

6c

Underline this idea above.

. . . .

Fortunately, we have found a buyer for your house at an excellent price. She will be away on business for two weeks, but when she returns, she has promised to effect a closing immediately. That means you will be receiving a check for about $68,000 in about three weeks. Congratulations!

6d

Rewrite the starting sentence of the above paragraph so that it not only tells the reader what the letter is about but includes the idea of most interest.

_____

_____

_____

. . . .

Congratulations! You will receive a check for about $68,000 in about three weeks because we have found a buyer for your house. (Congratulations!)

7a

Suppose you are writing a letter to an automobile dealer about a contemplated purchase of six new cars for your firm. Which of the following ideas should you include in your opening sentence? _____

A. a question about whether he has six cars in stock or will he have to order them from Detroit

B. that he has a reputation for honesty

C. that you need six new company cars

D. that the cars will be used by your salesmen

E. that he was referred to you by the district sales manager

F. that you are inviting a quotation of the best price he can offer

G. whether air-conditioning is available

H. that you are also writing to other dealers

. . . .

C and F

7b

Which of these states the purpose of your letter? _____ Which is of most interest to the dealer? _____

. . . .

    F
    C

7c

Write an opening sentence containing these two ideas.

_____

_____

_____

. . . .

I would like to invite you to quote us a price on six new cars which we need for company use.

8a

Which of the following opening sentences not only tells the reader what the letter is about but includes the item of most interest to him or her? _____

    A. Enclosed is our check for $1,500.

    B. Thank you for your letter explaining the delay in the delivery of the X48 Road-Grader.

    C. We are enclosing a sample copy of our weekly trade newsletter, "What's New in the Fur industry," which you can order for $6.50 on a six-month trial subscription basis.

. . . .

    C

8b

What is missing from Sentence A—an explanation of what the letter is about or a most interesting idea? _____

. . . .

    an explanation

8c

What is missing from Sentence B—an explanation of what the letter is about or a most interesting idea? _____

. . . .

    a most interesting idea

    (Sentence A is a bad opening, but Sentence B may be perfectly acceptable since there may not *be* an idea that is of special interest to the reader.)

9

When you are replying to a letter, it is customary to refer to the date of that letter in your starting sentence. Doing so makes it easier for your reader to consult the original letter if necessary. However, such reference should always be subordinated to what you are writing about. That is, do not devote the whole sentence to the date reference.

Which of the following four versions of an opening sentence is best?

A.   Thank you for your letter of May 16.

B.   I am enclosing the pamphlet you requested in your letter.

C.   Enclosed is the pamphlet you requested in your letter dated May 16.

D.   We received your letter of May 16 expressing interest in our pamphlet.

. . . .

C

(We realize that in some firms the custom is to refer to previous correspondence by writing the word "Re:" or "Subject:" and then the date or invoice number or whatever. This information is usually placed between the address and the salutation. If it is your organization's policy to do this, by all means follow that policy, but we will assume in this book that previous correspondence should be referred to in the body of the letter.)

10

I have received your order dated January 19. Your six shirts will be mailed within the week and should arrive before February 1 as you asked.

Rewrite the opening sentence.

_____

_____

_____

_____

. . . .

Your order, dated January 19, for six shirts will be mailed within the week and should arrive before February 1, as you asked.

or

Thank you for your order of January 19 for six shirts, which will be mailed within the week and should arrive before February 1, as you asked.

11a

Some letter writers have trouble getting started and consequently engage in a kind of verbal warm-up, which is usually full of clichés, generalizations, or ideas which are of no interest to the reader. For example:

I am sorry about the delay in answering your letter of March 2 but I was on vacation and have just returned. However, now that I'm back, your question is easily answered; yes, we do have a franchise available in southern Vermont.

Underline the _two_ ideas that should be included in the opening sentence of the above paragraph.

. . . .

I am sorry about the delay in answering your <u>letter of March 2</u> but I was on vacation and have just returned. However, now that I'm back, your question is easily answered; <u>yes, we do have a franchise available in southern Vermont.</u>

11b

Now write an opening sentence for this letter.

_____

_____

_____

. . . .

To (In) answer (to) your letter of March 2, yes, we do have a franchise available in southern Vermont.

12

Your opening sentences should contain:

1. an explanation of what your letter is about (including, sometimes, the purpose of the whole letter)

2. the idea of most interest to your reader, if possible

3. the date of your reader's letter, if applicable

Each of the starting sentences below lacks one or more of the above items. In each case, write the number or numbers of the missing items next to the sentence.

_____ A. Thank you for your kind letter of October 22.

_____ B. Enclosed is a copy of the speech you requested in your letter.

_____ C. I have finally been able to talk to Mr. Palmer about your plans and consequently have some good news for you.

. . . .

___1 and 2___ A.

____3____ B.

____2____ C.

13

Which of the following are good starting sentences? _____

A. As you asked in your letter of May 6, I am enclosing a copy of your article as it appeared in our September issue of "The Trackers Digest."

B. Thank you for your recent letter.

C. I have been going over the files for your account and am writing you about one of our invoices.

D. In the process of merging Georgia Carbide & Atlanta Steel, many of the executive personnel were forced to resign.

E. We have decided to advertise Gumshu on nationwide television and would like to know if you are interested in handling our account.

. . . .

A and E

(Sentence B does not tell the reader what the letter is about, nor does it refer to the date of the reader's letter; Sentence C is too vague; and Sentence D gives only the vaguest notion of what the letter is about.)

14

Suppose you are Director of Personnel and are answering a letter of inquiry, dated June 10, about openings in your company. The letter is from Joan L. Conrad, a recent college graduate who is interested in a managerial position. At the moment, only the job of traffic coordinator is open. The usual hiring procedure is for the applicant to submit an application and then an interview will be arranged.

Write an opening sentence for this letter:

Dear Ms. Conrad:

_____

_____

_____

. . . .

Your answer should include:

    1. the item of most interest to her: the position of traffic coordinator is open

    2. the date of her letter: June 10

In answer to your letter of June 10, we have a position as traffic coordinator open.

THE FINISH

15

One of the big problems for many letter writers is to think of something appropriate to say in closing. Thus they often end with a vague cliché which is as time-worn as it is insincere. Perhaps the first person who wrote, "Please do not hesitate to call on us if we can be of further assistance," really meant it, but today's readers have seen it so often that they barely notice such words.

Which of the following endings sounds sincere? _____

    A. May we again thank you for your cooperation in this matter.

    B. Thank you for returning the forms to me so quickly.

    C. Your prompt cooperation in expediting the above situation would be very much appreciated.

. . . .

    B

16a

One of the best ways to avoid the abstract cliché in closing a letter is to say something *specific*.

> Dear Mr. Martinez:
>
> Thank you for your order for fifty dozen LONGLITE batteries, which are being mailed via parcel post and should arrive no later than December 8.

Which of the following is the best ending for this letter? _____

    A. Please do not hesitate to call us if we can be of further service.

    B. Just give us a call if we can further assist you.

    C. Just give me a call when you need more batteries.

· ·

    C

16b

Which of the above endings is the worst? _____

· ·

    A

(Ending B above would be all right if Ending C were not better.)

17

Which of the following endings are acceptable? _____

    A. It has been a pleasure to be of assistance.

    B. Let me know if there is anything more I can do to help you with your financial affairs.

    C. May we have your check for $56.27 by June 16?

    D. If you have any further questions, do not hesitate to contact us.

    E. Trusting we will hear from you soon, I remain, . . .

· ·

    B and C

18a

While the first sentence of a business letter is a good place for putting the idea that is of paramount interest to the *reader*, the final sentence is the best place for expressing an idea that is of prime interest to the *writer*. The final sentence is usually the easiest for the reader to remember. Thus it offers an excellent opportunity for making a request for action, if that is the purpose of the letter.

Read the following just once:

> Please accept my apology for our error on Invoice #16853. Enclosed is our Invoice #17864 for thirty gross of wooden spools to replace the one you received for thirty-thousand gross. Please return the yellow copy with your payment.
>
> Because we just switched our billing over to a computer, we are still working out such bugs as the one which caused the extra zeros in your bill.
>
> Again, we are sorry for this mistake and will make every effort to see that it does not occur again.

Without going back, what specific action has the writer asked the reader to perform?

_____

. . . .

to return the yellow copy with his payment

(If you were not able to answer this, we are not surprised, since the request for action is well camouflaged.)

18b

Now go back and circle the request the writer has made and draw an arrow from the circle to the place where it should appear.

. . . .

Please accept my apology for our error on Invoice #16853. Enclosed is our Invoice #17864 for thirty gross of wooden spools to replace the one you received for thirty-thousand gross. (Please return the yellow copy with your payment.)

Because we just switched our billing over to a computer, we are still working out such bugs as the one which caused the extra zeros in your bill.

Again, we are sorry for this mistake and will make every effort to see that it does not occur again.

19

I'm sorry but the *Diary of Alfred S. Potts*, which you asked for in your letter of April 6, is no longer in print. However, we may be able to locate a used edition through our book-finding club which advertises in small magazines across the country. The charge for this service varies according to how many times we have to advertise but seldom amounts to more than $10.

Hoping to hear from you about this matter at your earliest convenience, I remain,

Yours Sincerely,

Rewrite this ending:

_____

_____

. . . .

If you do want the used edition, may we hear from you soon?

or

We will begin the search for your book as soon as we hear from you.

20

Below are sentences taken from a letter and put out of order. Which should come first? _____ Which should come last? _____

August 21

Mr. Thomas T. Evans
Director
Youth for Progress

Dear Mr. Evans:

A. Although our company has not up to now made any effort to locate or train personnel from the inner city, your report does suggest that we might find such a plan feasible.

B. Could you call me this week so that we can arrange to meet and discuss this further?

C. You mentioned also that you had information on the training staff and materials we would need to begin such a drive.

D. I read your letter of August 16 and your report with considerable interest, since I had not realized how much was being done in a practical way to prepare the underprivileged youths in our city to hold jobs in industry.

. . . .

D
B

21

Write a closing sentence for the following letter. You may extract information from the letter and use it in the closing sentence.

LEE'S DEPARTMENT STORE

Orange Tree Shopping Center

November 7

Mr. David Hicks
11 Maple Grove Street

Dear Mr. Hicks:

As you asked in your letter of November 5, I am enclosing an application for a charge account. However, because it takes approximately two weeks to process, please return it to us no later than the middle of this month to allow you ample time to use your account for your holiday shopping. We will call you when your application is approved and issue you a temporary shopping pass until your regular charge card can be made up.

. . . .

May we have your application, completed and signed, before November 15 (the middle of the month)?

22

When you are not requesting action from your reader but are simply supplying him or her with information, the ending of your letter is a good place to summarize your major points, especially if your letter is lengthy and detailed.

DR. HELEN E. BOUDREAU
Director of Research
Chicago Institute of Applied Psychology

April 15

Dr. T. E. Holland
State Mental Hospital

Dear Dr. Holland:

About your query in your letter of March 6, concerning our current research in hypnosis, we are currently conducting a series of experiments on the possible uses of hypnosis in medicine. Our experiment now under way involves twenty-five pairs of adults undergoing similar surgical operations at Chicago General Hospital. One patient in each pair receives an anesthetic before surgery and the other is hypnotized. We then compare them to determine if either method provides a faster convalescence and fewer postoperative complications.

A second experiment is being planned for mental patients currently in the care of the Illinois State Mental Hospitals. Again we will study matched pairs of adults, one to undergo psychoanalysis and the other hypnoanalysis, to compare the length of time required to return the patient to community life and the adequacy of adjustment.

And we are considering a third experiment to determine the feasibility of using hypnosis to re-educate and re-orient the alcoholic, drug addict, and habitual criminal to a more productive way of life.

Which of the following is the best ending to this letter? _____

A. I hope I have answered your question and will be glad to keep you posted on developments as they arise.

B. To summarize, then, we are currently looking into the possible uses of hypnosis for patients undergoing surgery, psychoanalysis, and social readjustment.

C. If you have further questions, please do not hesitate to call on me.

. . . .

B

23

Write the closing for the following:

AXON, TELLER & SEIBERT
Attorneys at Law
333 Madison Avenue

September 7

Mr. John T. Warner
President
Reco Combustion, Inc.

Dear Mr. Warner:

We met last week with Morris Filters' attorneys regarding your suit against them for breach of patent and tentatively agreed on an out-of-court settlement of $25,000. This seems reasonable to us, although, of course, if we prosecuted and won, we probably could get about twice that amount. The problem is that although you have a strong case, their attorneys tell us that they will request a jury trial, in which case the outcome is somewhat less certain than it would be if the case were heard before a judge.

Another consideration is the probable delay in bringing the suit to court. If Morris Filters wants, they can secure two or three postponements, after which, if we win the case, they can appeal to a higher court. Some of these patent cases have been known to take five or six years. If such were to happen, the consequent legal fees could leave you with less than the amount of the out-of-court settlement.

In conclusion, then, you can either accept the settlement of $25,000 or prosecute for about twice that at the risk of a jury trial and costly delays. We advise you to settle.

24

Complete the following letter:

JACKSON MAIL ORDERS, INC.
1148 14th Street N.W.

May 6

Ms. Cindy Williams
Vice President
Rotary Printing Co., Inc.

Dear Ms. Williams:

We are preparing a catalogue of our products and would like to receive your bid for printing, collating, and binding 250,000 copies. There will be approximately 108 5" × 7" pages, each with four illustrations; 48 pages in four-color half-tones and the remainder one-color; collated and saddle-stitched. As our mailing date is October 1, we would like to decide by the end of this month to allow three months to complete the catalogue.

_____

_____
. . . .

May we have your bid by May 30 (before the end of the month)?

_____

25

THE GREEN BAY LIFE INSURANCE COMPANY
Automobile Insurance Division
15 Terry Avenue

February 18

Mr. Peter Lowenthal
R. F. D. #1

Dear Mr. Lowenthal:

We have carefully considered your claim for $692.57 in repairs to your car which was damaged in your accident on February 3. Unfortunately, your policy lapsed on January 15, at the end of the thirty-day grace period which started immediately after the due date of your latest unpaid premium payment. During this grace period, we sent you two notices that your payment was overdue, but we did not hear from you. Consequently, your collision coverage lapsed and was not in effect when the accident occurred. Thus I am sorry we will not be able to reimburse you for the cost of repairing your car.

Which of the following is the best ending for this letter? _____

A. If I can be of any further service to you, please let me know.

B. In short, you have been uninsured since January 15.

C. If you wish to renew your policy, may I hear from you soon?

D. I am sorry this has happened, Mr. Lowenthal, especially since you have been a long-standing policy-holder with us, but I hope you will understand that we must stick to the precise wording of your policy agreement.

. . . .

D

(Sentence A is particularly inappropriate since the writer has been of no service at all. Sentence B is not necessary since the letter is fairly simple—it does not need a summary. Sentence C is asking the reader to be awfully reasonable, under the circumstances.)

This is the end of Lesson 5. Now turn to page 179 and take the Quiz for Lesson 5.

If your business letter is to be well organized, you must do some thinking and planning before you begin to write it. This does not mean that you should go through an elaborate procedure, especially if your letter is short and simple or if you have a large volume of correspondence to handle every day. But it does mean that some preparation is necessary for almost every letter you write.

Thus we recommend that you take the following three steps before you begin to actually write:

1. If you are replying to a letter, read it carefully and circle the important points you will cover in your own letter. Remember, your correspondent may not have been entirely clear, so you may have to read between the lines to get at what is really being expressed.

2. Take some time to familiarize yourself with the circumstances surrounding your letter. In other words, obtain as much background material as necessary. Get the file of the person to whom you are writing and read any past correspondence that bears on the present situation. It may help to discuss the case with others in your office who may be more familiar with it. Find out everything you can about your correspondent. Is he or she an old, influential customer? Does he or she have a record as a troublemaker? And so on. The small amount of time you spend on research can save you much time and expense later on.

3. Jot down in a short list the ideas you plan to include in your letter. Then go over your list and make sure you have included everything you want to say and exclude those ideas which are irrelevant. Juggle the ideas around and begin to think of where they will go in the letter. Which ideas do you want to include in your starting sentence? Which ones at the end? How should the body of the letter be laid out?

   (This step may not be necessary or practical if you are already an experienced correspondent with a heavy work load. However, for those who are beginners or who have trouble organizing their letters, a "laundry list" of ideas may be helpful.)

Once you have taken these three preparatory steps, you are ready to actually write the letter. At this point, the main object is to get it down. Let the ideas flow freely and don't worry about your sentence structure or about whether you are being wordy or using too many passive sentences.

After you have got it all out, let it sit for a while and cool off. If you are dictating the letter, have a draft copy made up. Few writers can be really objective about a letter which they have just written. So, once you have let some time go by, then sit down and revise the letter so that it becomes clear, concise, natural, courteous, and personal. (It already should be well organized.)

If you follow this procedure for each letter that you write, you will find that the need for revision will eventually diminish as you increase your writing skills. However, if you feel that this procedure is not practical during busy office hours, take home some of the copies of letters you have written during the day and increase your skill by revising them.

In the following lesson, we will give you practice in planning, writing, and revising some business letters.

REQUEST FOR AN ESTIMATE OF TIME AND COST

1a

Before we get into the process of planning and writing the letter, let's look at one that gives ample evidence that the writer engaged in little or no preparation before writing it. Read the following:

ARNOLD T. JACKLIN
Able Secretarial Service

June 8

Terminix Office Equipment, Inc.
57 Wytton Avenue

Dear Sirs:

(1) I recently purchased some used office furniture and equipment at a bankruptcy auction held last Thursday at a warehouse on Tremont Avenue. **(2)** In the lot, were some real bargains by way of office desks, chairs, etc. **(3)** Also in the lot I purchased was an old IBM electric typewriter. **(4)** As you probably know, these machines are pretty good if they are fixed up, and it appears that this one needs some work. **(5)** It looks like it has been stored in someone's attic for some time and probably needs a good cleaning. **(6)** What is your charge for this?

(7) By the way, one of my typists looked at it the other morning and told me that the ribbon does not wind properly and that the tab does not set. **(8)** In our line of work (secretarial service), we often do a lot of typing that requires the use of the tab. **(9)** How long do you think it would take to fix it?

(10) I am writing to several repair shops to get estimates for this job. **(11)** So I'd appreciate a prompt reply.

Look at Sentences 1 and 2. Do they give you a good idea of what the letter is about or what its purpose is? _____

. . . .

no

(They relate some information in which the reader will have little or no interest.)

1b

Look at Sentences 3, 4, 5, and 6. These sentences do tell the reader something of what the letter is about and what its purpose is, but they are also filled with several irrelevant ideas. Underline those parts that are pertinent to the business at hand.

. . . .

(3) Also in the lot I purchased was an <u>old IBM electric typewriter.</u> (4) As you probably know, these machines are pretty good if they are fixed up, and it appears that this one <u>needs some work.</u> (5) It looks like it has been stored in someone's attic for some time and probably <u>needs a good cleaning.</u> (6) <u>What is your charge for this?</u>

(The ideas that are not underlined should be thrown out.)

1c

Underline the parts of Sentences 7, 8, and 9 that should be included in a revision of the above letter.

. . . .

(7) By the way, one of my typists looked at it the other morning and told me that <u>the ribbon does not wind properly and that the tab does not set.</u> (8) In our line of work (secretarial service), we often do a lot of typing that requires the use of the tab. (9) <u>How long do you think it will take to fix it?</u>

1d

In Sentences 10 and 11, the writer finally states the purpose of his letter and makes a rather vague request for action. In summary, this letter is disorganized and ineffective because the writer has included a great many irrelevant ideas and has not placed the relevant ones in the right positions. To revise this letter, first jot down the ideas that should be included. Do not write full sentences.

1. _____

2. _____

3. _____

4. _____

5. _____

6. _____

. . . .

Your list does not have to be exactly like ours, but you should have included pretty much the same ideas.

1. old IBM electric typewriter—just acquired
2. needs cleaning and repairing
3. ribbon does not wind
4. tab does not set
5. cost?
6. how long?

1e

Using our list above, write a revised version of the first disorganized letter. Juggle the various parts in your mind. Which ideas should go in the opening sentence? What should go in the finish? (If you prefer, dictate the letter and have a draft copy typed.)

_____

_____

_____

_____

_____

_____

_____

_____

_____

_____

_____

_____

. . . .

Before you compare your revision with ours, go over it and make sure that it is clear, concise, natural, courteous, and personal.

Dear Sirs:

I would like to have your estimate for cleaning and repairing an old IBM electric typewriter. The ribbon does not wind properly and the tab does not set.

May we have your estimate as soon as possible for the cost of the above work and for the time it will take you to complete the job? Thank you.

Sincerely,

Estimate of Time and Cost

2a

Now suppose you are the owner of Terminix Office Equipment, Inc., and you have received the above letter from Mr. Jacklin of Able Secretarial Service. Below is a list of facts and thoughts which you have jotted down in order to reply to his letter:

1. charge for cleaning typewriter is flat fee: $35

2. his letter: wants estimate for cost and time to repair and clean used IBM (date June 8)

3. replacement of rewind mechanism: $6 to $8

4. if tab set must be rebuilt, cost is $20–$30; if repaired, $5–$10

5. free pickup and delivery

6. about two weeks to do the job

7. we have three repairmen experienced on IBM's and one experienced on Underwoods

8. high and low charge for cost estimate: $46–$73

9. we have complete stock of replacement parts

Two items in the above list represent ideas which are irrelevant to the purpose of the letter. Which are they? _____

. . . .

7 and 9

2b

Now begin to think of the ideas that will go into your starting sentence. Remember, you want it to tell your reader what your letter is about, to contain the idea(s) of most interest to him, and to refer to the date of his letter. Write the opening sentence.

_____

_____

_____

_____
. . . .

In reply to your letter of June 8, I estimate the cost for cleaning and repairing your used IBM typewriter at $46 to $73, and we should be able to deliver it in about two weeks.

2c

Now write the rest of the letter, except for the closing sentence.

_____

_____

_____

_____

_____

_____

_____

_____

_____

_____

_____

_____

_____

_____

· ·

We charge a flat fee of $25 for cleaning an electric typewriter. Replacement of the rewind mechanism will range from $6 to $8. If the tab set must be rebuilt, the cost is $20 to $30, but if it only needs repair, the cost is $5 to $10.

2d

Now write a finish for this letter which is as specific as you can make it.

_____

_____

_____

_____

· ·

We have a free pickup and delivery service and will be glad to come and get your typewriter as soon as we hear from you.

A CHANGE OF PLANS

3a

Suppose you are the manager of a new research project for a large pharmaceutical company. The goal of the project is to develop drugs to be used during and after open heart surgery. Your laboratory is in Annapolis, Maryland, but the home office of your firm is in Oakland, California. For the past few months, you have been trying to persuade Dr. Elvin S. Maynard, a brilliant but temperamental scientist, to move his family down from Cambridge, Massachusetts, to Annapolis and join your research team. In previous correspondence, you had arranged for him to bring his family down on July 10, 11, and 12 for an outing in the Annapolis area and for Dr. Maynard to inspect your facilities and meet other members of your team. You had planned to be at the airport yourself to meet his flight (510—American Airlines) at 11:30 a.m. on the 10th. Unfortunately, you have just been ordered to make a presentation of your project's aims and accomplishments to the Board of Directors in Oakland and will be away during the 10th and 11th, although you may be able to make it back on the morning of the 12th. Thus there are two possibilities: Dr. Maynard can come down as arranged, and Dr. Ellen Fastner, your Head Researcher, can take your place as host, or Dr. Maynard's trip can be postponed.

You are sitting down to write Dr. Maynard of the recent developments and to explain the alternatives. First, you jot down the ideas you want to include in your letter, as follows:

1. sorry, can't meet you at airport as planned on July 10

2. your flight: 510—American Airlines due 11:30 a.m.

3. just been called to Oakland home office

4. make presentation of project's aims and accomplishments to Board of Directors

5. can't get out of it; it's a command performance

6. two alternatives

7. postpone your trip a few days

8. or Dr. Ellen Fastner takes my place as your host

9. she is Head Researcher

10. will try to get back on the morning of the 12th

11. can do so by flying all night

12. can at least have a talk before you go back

13. let me know what you want to do

Cross off any ideas in this list which should not be included in the letter.

. . . .

You should have crossed out ideas 2, 5, and 11.

(Idea 2 represents information that the reader already knows. Idea 5 is really not relevant because the very fact that the presentation is for the Board of Directors indicates the necessity of making it. Idea 11 is a little dramatic and might unduly influence Dr. Maynard's decision about what to do.)

3b

1. sorry, can't meet you at airport as planned on July 10

2. ~~your flight: 510—American Airlines due 11:30 a.m.~~

3. just been called to Oakland home office

4. make presentation of project's aims and accomplishments to Board of Directors

5. ~~can't get out of it; it's a command performance~~

6. two alternatives

7. postpone your trip a few days

8. or Dr. Ellen Fastner takes my place as your host

9. she is Head Researcher

10. will try to get back on the morning of the 12th

11. ~~can do so by flying all night~~

12. can at least have a talk before you go back

13. let me know what you want to do

Now begin to consider the above list of ideas in relation to the letter you will write. Which ones will go into your starting sentence? Your closing? Remember, you are very anxious to hire Dr. Maynard, so you want to present yourself and your firm in the best light.

Now write a draft of your letter and set it aside for five or ten minutes. Then edit it so that it is as clear, concise, natural, courteous, and personal as you can make it. (If you prefer, dictate the letter and have a draft copy typed.)

_____

_____

_____

_____

_____

_____

Dear Dr. Maynard:

I'm very sorry but I will not be able to meet you at the airport on the morning of July 10, as we had arranged. Unfortunately, I have just been called to our home office in Oakland, California, on the 10th to make a presentation of the project's aims and accomplishments to the Board of Directors.

It seems to me that there are two alternatives: you can postpone your trip down here for a few days, or, if you would prefer, you can come down with your family as planned. Dr. Ellen Fastner, my Head Researcher, would be happy to take my place as your host for the 10th and 11th, and I will try to get back on the morning of the 12th so that we can have a chat before you return to Cambridge.

Please let me know what you prefer to do, and I will make the appropriate arrangements.

Sincerely,

SALVAGING GOODWILL

4a

One of the most difficult tasks that you must face as a business letter writer is that of turning down readers and still keeping their goodwill for your firm. No one likes to be refused, but sometimes you can salvage the reader's goodwill if your letter is as positive, reasonable, and sympathetic as you can make it. Here are several devices and techniques for making it so:

1. The first thing the reader wants to know from a refusal letter is "why?" Thus it is extremely important that you give specific *reasons* for the refusal—when you can. Sometimes, of course, it may be necessary to keep the reason for the refusal secret, but most of the time you will be able to explain your decision in detail. This explanation should come *before* the actual refusal—to soften the blow. Above all, do not appeal to "company policy" as the sole reason for the turn-down. This usually infuriates readers because their natural reaction is, "Why is company policy the way it is? You're just evading the issue." Remember, most people will respond positively to an appeal to their most reasonable selves.

2. Assure your readers that you have carefully considered their requests (or complaints) by saying so and by making your letters *specific* enough so that they apply only to each reader's situation. Doing this will demonstrate that you and your firm care enough to take a little longer.

3. When you can, offer your readers *positive alternatives.* Often situations are not totally hopeless and there are suggestions you can make to help readers over their disappointment.

Below is a letter which says *no* to the reader. It contains examples of some of the techniques and devices described above. Read the letter and write the number of the device or technique next to the part that exemplifies it.

ALEXANDER UNIVERSITY

May 11

Mr. James F. Depolo
10 Rivington Road

Dear Mr. Depolo:

_____ { Our Entrance Board has carefully considered your application to our Liberal Arts School.

_____ { Mrs. Ewing, who interviewed you in February, was much impressed with your maturity and composure and gave you her enthusiastic endorsement before the Board. However, the Board noted that your high-school grades in English and French were below the standards we require, as were your scores on the language skills parts of the Scholastic Achievement Test. We have found over the years that in order for you to have an even chance to succeed in any of the Liberal Arts programs, you would need a higher degree of language and writing skills than you now possess. Thus I am sorry that we cannot accept you next Fall in the Liberal Arts College.

_____ { However, I notice that you have a superior record in math and science. Perhaps, if you resubmitted your application to our Mechanical Engineering School, the Board would look more favorably on it. Or, if you are determined to take a liberal arts program, there is still plenty of time to apply at such fine institutions as Albany College in Rumston, Virginia, or Arlington College in Feldspar, Maryland, where the language skills requirements are more suited to your abilities.

Good luck.

Sincerely,

. . . .

2
1
3

4b

Note the part of the letter which gives the reasons for the refusal. Does the actual refusal come before or after the reasons? _____

. . . .

after

(The blow of the actual turn-down is somewhat softened if the reasons for it precede it.)

REFUSAL OF AN ORDER

5a

Suppose you are the Manager of the Publications Division of The American Stockbrokers Association, a nonprofit trade organization for brokerage firms with about eight hundred members across the country. You have received an order for fifty copies of one of your publications, a book called *Analyzing Financial Statements*, from Ms. Corine Melillo, Vice-President in the Credit Department, Peat-Warmouth Manufacturing Co., Inc., Pittsburgh, Pennsylvania, who wrote, "I have read this book, and I want every employee in my department to have a copy."

Because your organization is a nonprofit trade association, it is regulated by Federal law, which says that you can sell your publications only to your members—the eight hundred or so brokerage firms. Thus you must return Ms. Melillo's order unfilled. Nevertheless, you look at the list of your members and discover that there are two in Pittsburgh: Johnson, Phipps & Keys, Inc., and L. F. Rothschild & Co., Inc. It is possible for Ms. Melillo to ask them to order the books for her.

First you jot down the ideas you want to include in your letter:

1. have carefully considered your letter

2. thanks for the order

3. am returning your order

4. fifty copies of *Analyzing Financial Statements*

5. we are nonprofit trade association—with eight hundred members

6. Federal law says we can sell only to members

7. two member brokerage houses in Pittsburgh: Johnson, Phipps & Keys, Inc., and L. F. Rothschild & Co., Inc.

8. have them order

9. be glad to fill it

Cross out any of the ideas above that should not be included in your letter.

. . . .

You should have crossed out idea 1, since there is very little to consider. Federal law has made your decision for you. All you are doing is following it. Thus it would be slightly untruthful to say, "I have carefully considered your letter." Also, you would not be entirely incorrect if you crossed out idea 4, since the reader may already know what her order consisted of. However, we think it should stay so that it may be used to identify the reader's order for her beyond a doubt.

5b

Now write your letter of refusal to Ms. Melillo. (If you prefer, dictate the letter and have a draft copy typed.)

_____

_____

_____

_____

_____

_____

_____

_____

_____

_____

_____

_____

_____

_____

_____

_____

_____

_____

_____

_____

_____

_____

_____

_____

_____

_____

_____

_____

_____

. . . .

Before you compare your letter with ours, edit it to make it clear, concise, natural, courteous, and personal.

Dear Ms. Melillo:

Thank you for your order for fifty copies of *Analyzing Financial Statements.* As a nonprofit trade association for brokerage firms with about eight hundred members across the country, we are regulated by Federal law, which stipulates that we sell our publications to our members only. Therefore, I regretfully must return your order unfilled.

However, I notice that there are two of our member firms in Pittsburgh: Johnson, Phipps & Keys, Inc., and L. F. Rothschild & Co., Inc. I'm sure that either of them would be happy to order the books for you.

Sincerely,

ONE LAST WORD

Now that you have worked through the six lessons of this book, we hope that you will begin to apply some of the writing principles and skills that you have learned. For it is only through a constant effort of will and by continual practice that the writing of better business letters will become second nature to you. We cannot hope to make you an expert in the short time you have been working in this book, but you should have taken a large step toward becoming one.

Even more important, we hope that you have developed the right outlook toward the job of writing letters. Business letter writing does not necessarily have to be a burdensome chore. Rather we hope you will see the business letter as an effective medium for carrying forward your own career and for conducting the business of your firm. With this in mind, here is a useful piece of advice from Sir Ernest Gowers, who wrote some time ago:

> Be sure that you know what your correspondent is asking before you begin to answer him. Study his letter carefully. If he is obscure, spare no trouble in trying to get at his meaning. If you conclude that he means something different from what he says (as he well may), address yourself to his meaning not to his words, and do not be clever at his expense.

> Get into his skin, and adapt the atmosphere of your letter to suit that of his. If he is troubled, be sympathetic. If he is rude, be specially courteous. If he is muddle-headed, be specially lucid. If he is pig-headed, be patient. If he is helpful, be appreciative. If he convicts you of a mistake, acknowledge it freely and even with gratitude. But never let a flavour of the patronising creep in.

Now turn to page 183 and take the Quiz for Lesson 6.

APPENDIX
BUSINESS-LETTER LAYOUT AND OTHER CONVENTIONS

Your reader's total impression of you and your firm, for good or ill, is formed not only by the contents of your letter but by the way it looks. Thus, to help make a good impression, your letters should be neatly and accurately typed on attractive stationery, have the proper layout, and conform to all other business-letter conventions.

This appendix demonstrates three common types of letter layout and covers the conventions that pertain to the various parts of business letters. Before reading any further, however, you should refer to your firm's letter-writing guidebook or handbook (if one exists). If there are any differences between it and this appendix, you should, of course, ignore what we say here.

LETTER LAYOUT

Although most authorities would agree that there is no one "correct" business-letter layout, they usually recognize three basic forms:

1. *Semiblock form* is a middle-of-the-road layout used by most organizations. It is easy to type and has a modern appearance that does not call attention to itself.

2. *Block form* is the most modern and is the quickest and easiest to type.

3. *Modified block form* combines some of the features of both semiblock and block forms.

On the following pages are examples of the three letter-layout forms.

SEMIBLOCK FORM

JAMES M. REID COMPANY
COOPER HILL ROAD
RIDGEFIELD, CONNECTICUT 06877
(203) 438-7792

Training Materials • *Programmed Instruction* • *Textbooks* • *Professional Writing*

January 1, 1978

Mr. John Q. Letterwriter
President
Letterwriting Enterprises, Inc.
1120 Avenue of the Americas
New York, New York 10020

Dear Mr. Letterwriter: Subject: Letter Layout

    This letter is an example of the standard semiblock form of
letter layout.

    Note that the date, subject line (Semiblock Letter Layout),
complimentary close, and signature section are aligned at the same
tab stop and that the first line of each paragraph is indented.

    As you can see, the semiblock form is popular because it is
attractive and easy to type. The typist simply sets standard
margins and tab stops and never has to change them.

                    Sincerely yours,

                    James M. Reid, Jr.
                    Co-author, Better Business Letters

JMR:as

Mr. John Q. Letterwriter - Page 2 January 1, 1978

    This is an example of a continuation page in the semiblock
format. Notice that the same standard margins and tab stops as
those on the first page of the letter are used.

    The addressee's name and the date are repeated at the top just
in case the second page should become separated from the first.

                           Sincerely yours,

                           James M. Reid, Jr.
                           Co-author, <u>Better Business Letters</u>

JMR:as

BLOCK FORM

JAMES M. REID COMPANY
COOPER HILL ROAD
RIDGEFIELD, CONNECTICUT 06877
(203) 438-7792

Training Materials • Programmed Instruction • Textbooks • Professional Writing

January 1, 1978

Mr. John Q. Letterwriter
President
Letterwriting Enterprises, Inc.
1120 Avenue of the Americas
New York, New York 10020

Dear John:

This letter is an example of the standard block form--the most
modern of the business-letter layouts. It is also the least
used but is gaining in popularity because it is easy and fast
for the typist.

As you can see, everything is flush left on the margin. The
inside address and paragraphs are single-spaced, even though the
letter is quite short, with double spaces between paragraphs.

Sincerely,

James M. Reid, Jr.
Co-author, Better Business Letters

JMR:as

MODIFIED BLOCK FORM

James M. Reid, Jr.
Cooper Hill Road
Ridgefield, Connecticut 06877

January 1, 1978

Mr. John Q. Letterwriter
President
Letterwriting Enterprises, Inc.
1120 Avenue of the Americas
New York, New York 10020

Dear John:

This modified block form is quite popular among students and others
who are writing business letters on stationery not having a letterhead. It is also widely used by organizations that <u>do</u> have a letterhead centered at the top.

Notice that it is the same as the block form, except that the date
and signature section are on the right, as in the semiblock form.

                          Best,

                          James M. Reid, Jr.
                          Co-author, <u>Better Business Letters</u>

JMR:as

PARTS OF THE LETTER

The Heading

The heading consists of the writer's complete address, date, and sometimes the name and title of the writer. The address should always include the zip code. Below are two examples of headings:

Darnell Industries, Inc.
4821 Crowswood Avenue
Chicago, Illinois 60640

Anthony M. Velotta, Treasurer

January 1, 1978

- -

Tomkins and Holik
Attorneys-at-Law
100684 Topanga Boulevard
Los Angeles, California 90052

Helen F. Tomkins
Catherine Holik
Maria T. Perez
Jules Lang

Telephone
858–6170
Area Code 213

January 1, 1978

Note the form of the date above. It is the only correct form. The following are not correct.

Incorrect: Jan. 1, 1978
1/1/78
January 1st, 1978

The Inside Address

The inside address of the reader should be exactly the same as the address on the envelope.

If the addressee is male, write "Mr." or his personal title—with his official title below, as shown below:

Mr. Thorsten F. Krone
Assistant Treasurer

Dr. Wilbur F. Oates
Director of Surgery

If the addressee is female, write "Ms.," "Miss," or "Mrs.," or her personal title, as shown below:

Ms. Alice P. Stietzel
President

Mrs. Helen G. Turner
Special Assistant

Dr. Linn Harding
Director of Research

Names of titles, streets, cities, and states should be spelled out. Be sure to include the zip code.

Correct	Incorrect
Mr. Robert Loring	Mr. Robt. Loring
Vice President	VP
Haley Publishing Company, Inc.	Haley Publishing Company
1650 Seventh Avenue	1650 7th Ave.
New York, New York 10017	New York, N. Y.

The Salutation

The salutation in a business letter is *always* followed by a colon, even if you use only the reader's first name. Below are the most common types of salutations:

Dear Mr. McDevitt:	Gentlemen:
Dear Miss Galloway:	Ladies:
Dear Dr. Hartman:	Dear Sir:
Dear Don:	Dear Sirs:

Always use the reader's name in the salutation, if you know it. When you do not have a specific name, write "Gentlemen" or "Dear Sirs"—unless the organization is primarily female.

The Subject Line

Some organizations require that a subject line be included in all letters, to tell the reader quickly what the letter is about. It is particularly appropriate when you are writing in reference to something that has a number, such as an invoice or an account.

With the semiblock style, the subject line is placed to the right of the last line of the inside address (see page 152). With block and modified block styles, it goes between the inside address and the salutation, as shown below:

Ajax Auto Supplies, Inc.
118 West Peach Street
Atlanta, Georgia 30301

Invoice #1287654 ◄——————— SUBJECT LINE

Gentlemen:

The Complimentary Close

If your letter is to a stranger, the following closes are appropriate:

Yours truly,
Yours very truly,

If you are writing to someone you know quite well, the following closes are more friendly:

Sincerely yours,	Cordially yours,
Sincerely,	Best,

Do not use stilted or cute closings, such as:

Yours in haste,	Yours till the cows come home,
Very faithfully yours,	Your obedient servant,

And do not attach such phrases as "I remain . . . " or "We are . . . " to the end of the body of your letter.

The Signature

Your signature may take various forms, depending on your organization's policy and what is in your letterhead.

If your name and title are in the letterhead, then only your signature is sufficient, as in:

Sincerely yours,

Ronald F. Porter

If your name and title are not in the letterhead, the following is correct:

Sincerely yours,

Ronald F. Porter

Ronald F. Porter
Office Manager

Some organizations want to have their names in the signature also, as in:

Sincerely yours,

THE GREEN COMPANY

Ronald F. Porter

Ronald F. Porter
Office Manager

Sincerely yours,

Ronald F. Porter

Ronald F. Porter
Office Manager
THE GREEN COMPANY

It's good practice for women to indicate, under their signature, how they wish to be addressed.

Jane D. Fowler

(Miss) Jane D. Fowler

Felicity N. Gates

Felicity N. Gates
(Mrs. John T. Gates)

Initials

The initials of the writer and typist are usually placed flush with the left margin, slightly below the signature. The writer's initials precede the colon; the typist's follow it. For example:

JMR:lh   JMR:LH   jmr:lh

Enclosures

Enclosures are indicated by writing the word "Enclosures" or the abbreviations "Encl." or "Enc." below the initials. If there is more than one enclosure, add the number. Examples:

Enclosures 2   Encl. 4

Copies

If copies (cc is the abbreviation) of the letter are to be sent to others besides the reader, include an entry such as the following:

JMR:lh   JMR:lh

Enc. 3   Enc. 3

Copies to: Mrs. Patricia Marlow   cc: Mr. A. Pomeroy
                  Commander F. Wright Davis   Miss Williams

THE USE OF NUMBERS

There is some disagreement among experts concerning the way numbers should be expressed in business letters. Nevertheless, this section provides some simple rules about the use of numbers, with emphasis on *consistent* usage.

Generally, you should spell out numbers that can be expressed in one or two words; use figures for numbers that require more than two words. Below are some examples:

<u>Words:</u>	one	twenty	one hundred
	two	twenty-one	two thousand
	ten	fifty-two	thirty thousand
	eleven	ninety-nine	five million

<u>Figures:</u>	101		10,100
	563		21,000
	1400	(fourteen hundred)	286,508
	1403		11,446,000

Notice the commas between the hundreds, thousands, and millions.

If a number appears at the beginning of a sentence, you should spell it out or revise the sentence so that the number is not first.

<u>Inappropriate:</u>   341 tons of raw cotton were shipped.

<u>Appropriate:</u>   Three hundred forty-one tons of raw cotton were shipped.

or

We shipped 341 tons of raw cotton.

Use figures when presenting numbers in a series.

Inconsistent:	This year, the Milburn Insurance Company hired 156 clerks, ninety-one typists, and fourteen receptionists.
Consistent:	This year, the Milburn Insurance Company hired 156 clerks, 91 typists, and 14 receptionists.

Always use figures when dates are involved.

Correct:	July 10, 1978
	July 10
Incorrect:	July tenth, 1978
	July 10th, 1978

Always use figures in street numbers. Commas are *not* used between the hundreds and thousands.

Correct:	383 Madison Avenue
	2316 Commonwealth Avenue
	10900 Ventura Boulevard

Pages and sections of books are always in figures.

Correct:	page 162, pages 162–184
	Chapter 8
	Lesson 21
	Part IV

Decimals and percentages are always in figures.

Correct:	In college, she had an average of 4.9 out of 5.
	60 percent or 60%
	31.8 percent or 31.8%

Hours are always in figures when used with *a.m.* or *p.m.* They are spelled out when used with *o'clock.*

Correct:	10 a.m. (ten o'clock in the morning)
	11:14 p.m.

DIAGNOSTIC TEST

Name: _____   Date: _____

This Diagnostic Test is designed to detect various aspects of your letter-writing skills that need some improvement. The various sections of the test are coordinated with the six lessons of the book, so that if your score is below par in any one section, you can work through the associated lesson to upgrade your skills in that area.

Please answer the following items carefully.

The five sentences below contain unnecessary words and phrases or wordy expressions which can cause business letters to be verbose. Cross out all unnecessary words or phrases. If an expression is wordy but cannot be eliminated without changing the meaning of the sentence, cross it out and replace it with a more concise expression.

1. Our operators were not able to complete some long distance calls because of the fact that transmission cables were out at about five or six of our installations.

2. I personally feel that our advertising campaign should be designed along the lines that I outlined in my letter under date of March 22.

3. Our factory, which is located in Bellevue, has been shut down for retooling purposes but should begin producing again at an early date.

4. In order to receive your certificate, you must complete a course on the basic fundamentals of cost accounting.

Some writers of business letters use general words when more specific words would increase the conciseness and clarity of their sentences. The following three sentences contain general words which prevent them from carrying their fair share of meaning. Underline these general words.

5. A 6 percent increase in sales was achieved in the Western District.

6. In May, there was a measurable change in the weather, indicating that the cloud-seeding program may have been worthwh'

7. When you reach Amarillo, our regior   ᵤsentative will get in contact with you and try to effect a ⌐   ᵤnt of your accounts.

Another problem with ⌐   ᵤetters is that too many of the sentences contain predicates in th⌐   ᵤᵤ, which make the letters weak and wordy. Put a check mark ᵣ⌐   ᵤntence below that contains a predicate in the passive voice and ᵤᵤ so that the predicate is in the active voice.

_____ 8. This shipment to us was received on June 10.

_____

_____   _____

_____ 9. Mr. McGraw is the ᵢᵢ.   vee to receive benefits under our new company health-care plan.

_____

_____

_____ 10. I will phone you as soon as the job is finished by the consᵤ

_____

_____

_____ 11. Diversification of our product line was delayed by lack of capital.

_____

_____

_____ 12. You may be assured that I will give you all the help I can.

_____

_____

Writers of better business letters always insert links (coordinating conjunctions, con-
junctive adverbs, transitional expressions, etc.) in their sentences so that their readers
can better understand the relationships between the ideas expressed. In the following
sentences, insert the appropriate link to show the relationship between the ideas.

Example: He is a slow ___but___ careful worker.

13. We have finished our analysis of work flow in the Receivables Department

_____ have started to draw up a list of recommendations

for improvement.

14. Norprop, Inc. will soon have several job openings, _____

their sales force is expanding.

15. The new clause concerning forfeits does not really give your client full

protection. It does, _____, make it more difficult for

irresponsible parties to sue her.

16. Our production manager was not informed of the October increase in sales.

_____, the factory had to go on triple shift in November

to meet the influx of orders.

17. We can send you a check for $50 as a refund, _____ we can

credit this amount to your account.

Parallelism is a useful device for bringing order and clarity to your writing. However, it should be used correctly. Put a check mark next to each sentence below which contains a mistake in the use of parallelism and revise the sentence to correct the mistake.

_____ 18. I wanted not only to find out what went wrong but also I asked the manager to assure us that it would not happen again.

_____

_____

_____

_____ 19. You may choose Plan A, which is less costly, but more inconvenient, or Plan B, which is more costly but less inconvenient.

_____

_____

_____

_____ 20. This offer had a twofold purpose—to stimulate dealer sales and the education of individual customers.

_____

_____

_____

_____ 21. All our operatives are given instruction in handling investigations and how to analyze data.

_____

_____

_____ 22. To stimulate higher gross sales is not necessarily making a higher profit.

_____

_____

A common fault of many business letters is the over-use of inflated language, archaic usage, negative words, and an impersonal tone. In the following sentences, cross out such mistakes and write your revisions over them.

_____ 23. Subsequent to our meeting, I had a long talk with Mr. Abrams with refer-

ence to your application and regret to inform you that he did not approve

it.

_____ 24. In the event that the assignment is completed satisfactorily, I will send you

a bill pursuant to our agreement of May 10.

_____ 25. It is impossible for delivery of the station wagon to be made until about a

week after Christmas.

_____ 26. Enclosed herewith please find a new contract, which you should duly note,

affix your signature thereto, and return to this office.

Please answer the following questions concerning the opening and closing sentences of business letters.

_____ 27. Is the following sentence an acceptable way to open a business letter? _____

I have received your letter of June 20.

_____ 28. What should be the *primary* objective of the opening sentence of a business letter?

_____

_____

_____ 29. In your opening sentence, you should try to include the idea which is most interesting to [you/the reader].

_____ 30. Is the following sentence a good way to open a business letter? _____

Our company is in the process of deciding on a location for one of our branch stores.

_____ 31. If you are replying to a letter, why is it a good idea to include a reference to the date of that letter in your opening sentence?

_____

_____

_____ 32. Is the following sentence an acceptable way to close a business letter? _____

Please do not hesitate to call on us if we may be of further assistance.

_____ 33. In the closing sentence of a letter, you should include the idea which is of most interest to [you/your reader].

_____ 34. Is the following sentence an acceptable way to close a business letter?

_____

Please return the sample to me by January 18.

_____ 35. The end of a business letter is a good place to do two things. What are they?

a. _____

b. _____

Please answer the following questions concerning the writing of the business letter as a whole.

_____ 36. What are *three* things you can do to prepare yourself *before* actually starting to write a business letter?

a. _____

b. _____

c. _____

_____ 37. One of the most difficult tasks that letter-writers face is that of turning down a reader's request or application and still salvaging the reader's goodwill. What are *three* things you can do to salvage the reader's goodwill when writing a turn-down letter?

a. _____

b. _____

c. _____

_____ 38. What are the *two* main purposes of drawing up a "laundry list" of ideas that you plan to include in a letter you wish to write?

a. _____

b. _____

_____ 39. Should the reasons for a turn-down come *before* or *after* the actual turn-down sentence? _____

_____ 40. Besides actually saying it, what is another way of showing the reader that you have given his or her request careful consideration?

_____

_____

If you are working through this book on your own, you may score your Diagnostic Test according to the correct answers on page 187.

If not, your instructor will have the answers to the Diagnostic Test.

QUIZ FOR LESSON 1

NAME: _____ DATE: _____

In the letter below, cross out all unnecessary or redundant words or phrases and write in appropriate revisions where required. There are *ten* changes in all.

THE ACME FINANCE COMPANY, INC.
118 Orange Grove Avenue

January 28

Ms. Helen Williams
Williams Collection Agency
16 Willard Street

Dear Ms. Williams:

Please be advised that we do not in the normal course of procedure use independent collection agencies. However, due to the fact that each and every one of your references has given you an excellent report, I am asking you to take one of our more difficult cases, which is that of Mr. Browning. In the last six months, we have sent him five overdue notices in connection with his automobile installment payments but have not heard from him.

As a consequence of this, I am sending you his installment-loan contract and other pertinent data, hoping you will have better success in collecting it at an early date.

I personally think that if you can resolve this case to our satisfaction, you can expect some more business from us in about two or three weeks.

Sincerely,

Clark H. Healy

If you are working through this book on your own, you may score your Quiz according to the correct answers on page 194.

If not, your instructor will have the answers to the Quiz.

QUIZ FOR LESSON 2

NAME: _____ DATE: _____

Complete each of the following five sentences with the most *specific* word or phrase by writing the letter of your choice in the space provided.

1. Please be sure to sign the application _____.

   A. in the lower left-hand corner
   B. in the appropriate place
   C. near the bottom

2. You may expect your order to arrive in Detroit _____.

   A. in about ten days
   B. soon
   C. on January 10

3. Ms. Phelps has made a _____ contribution to the field of electronics.

   A. significant
   B. revolutionary
   C. worthwhile

4. As soon as we obtain the necessary information, Mr. Klein will _____ you.

   A. communicate with
   B. get in touch with
   C. phone

5. Miss Lawson does seem to have a legitimate claim against the factory since the sidewalk in front of the main gate was _____ last Monday morning.

   A. unsafe
   B. icy
   C. hazardous

Rewrite each of the following passive sentences so that it becomes *active.* If the verb is *general*, replace it with a more specific one. You may have to make up a plausible doer of the action in some cases.

6. Completion of the project will be accomplished by the contractor before next June.

7. Production at the Yuma plant has not been seriously hampered by the earthquake.

_____

_____

8. Five copies of the manuscript were received two weeks ago.

_____

_____

9. The following letter from an instrument manufacturer's service manager to a customer who has asked for service on her Model M−2 spectroscope contains some passive sentences. Revise the letter by changing *all* passive sentences to active ones.

PRECISION INSTRUMENT CORPORATION
10116 110th Street, N. W.

September 16

Miss Pauline Whitman
Quality Control Department
Morris Corporation

Dear Miss Whitman:

I am sorry to hear that you have been having difficulties with your M−2 spectroscope. The problem has been turned over by me to Harry Masten, our serviceman for your area; and you will be phoned by him this week to schedule a service call.

I realize that your M−2 spectroscope must be operating to specifications by next Monday in order to maintain your production schedule. Mr. Masten also understands this, and the necessary repairs will be made by him when he arrives at your plant.

Arrangements should be made by you to have a purchase order number ready for

Mr. Masten to prevent further delay in accomplishing these repairs.

Sincerely,

If you are working through this book on your own, you may score your Quiz according to the correct answers on page 196.

If not, your instructor will have the answers to the Quiz.

QUIZ FOR LESSON 3

NAME: _____ DATE: _____

Fill in the appropriate links in the following:

1. The new production-line machines are more efficient _____
   more economical than the old machines.

2. We hope to have our hotel open for business by July 4th, _____
   we will not know for certain until at least the middle of May.

3. I advise you to put extra cash in tax-exempt bonds _____
   in a savings account, but not both.

4. Allied Mills, Inc. has been a valuable and reliable customer over the years.
   Lately, _____, they have become increasingly slow in paying
   their bills.

5. All our life insurance policies have a grace period of thirty days in which a
   late premium may be paid without the policy's lapsing. Unfortunately, we
   did not receive your payment until fifteen days after the grace period
   expired. _____, your policy has lapsed and you will have
   to undergo a medical examination if you wish to renew coverage.

The following sentences contain faults in parallelism. Correct them.

6. All line supervisors in the Home Office will be given training in applying
   the latest management techniques and how to interpret production data.

7. The clerks we hired from the Office Temporaries Corporation are courteous,
   efficient, and work hard.

8. We have a plan in the works not only for expanding sales by 10% next year but also to increase profits by 20%.

9. Mr. Feenan interviewed the executives of Viceroy Company, Inc. on Tuesday, flew back to the office on Wednesday, and his report was submitted to me on Thursday.

10 I received your order for three Model X−54 earthmovers on July 22, and it was immediately sent by me to our sales representative in your territory.

If you are working through this book on your own, you may score your Quiz according to the correct answers on page 198.

If not, your instructor will have the answers to the Quiz.

QUIZ FOR LESSON 4

NAME: _____ DATE: _____

The following sentences contain examples of inflated language, archaic usage, negative words, and an impersonal tone. Cross them out and write in your revisions over them.

1. It is deemed advisable that you file your Declaration of Estimated Tax prior to January 21.

2. As was requested by you in your letter of June 11, please find herewith enclosed a summary of the net worth accounts.

3. As per our agreement, I am enclosing a check for $2,000.

4. It is impossible for us to install your computer before next month sometime.

5. Immediately subsequent to the Bankers Committee meeting last Friday, this writer talked privately with John Masters with reference to a promotion for you.

6. It is always a pleasure to hear that someone like yourself has been promoted to Vice President.

If you are working through this book on your own, you may score your Quiz according to the correct answers on page 199.

If not, your instructor will have the answers to the Quiz.

QUIZ FOR LESSON 5

NAME: _____ DATE: _____

1a. Revise the *opening sentence* for the following letter. You may use information from the whole letter, but your answer should consist of only *one* opening sentence.

NEWTOWN NATIONAL BANK

January 10

Miss Francine Palazzo
R. F. D. #1

Dear Miss Palazzo:

I received your letter of January 6. In it you requested a refund of interest you paid on Note #6178. It seems our Note Teller calculated the interest using the higher interest rate instead of the lower one. I have looked into the matter and learned that you were perfectly right. He should have used the lower rate. Accordingly, I am enclosing a check for $56.28, representing the difference.

_____

_____

_____

_____

_____

1b. Now write the *closing sentence* for the above letter. Again, you may use information from the rest of the letter, but your answer should consist of only *one* closing sentence.

_____

_____

_____

_____

_____

_____

2. Revise the *opening sentence* for the following. You may use parts of the whole example, but your answer should consist of only *one* opening sentence.

I would have answered your letter of October 25 sooner, but it has just arrived at my desk. In answer to your question about employment with us, we do expect an opening for an optical technician to occur in about six months.

_____

_____

_____

_____

_____

3. Revise the *closing sentence* for the following. You may use parts of the whole example, but your answer should consist of only *one* closing sentence.

Thank you for your order of thirty West-Tec air-conditioners, Model #461. We have shipped them via Railway Express, and they should arrive in St. Louis by September 4. If we can be of further service, please do not hesitate to call on us.

_____

_____

_____

_____

_____

4. Revise the *closing sentence* for the following. You may use parts of the whole example, but your answer should consist of only *one* closing sentence.

I want to coordinate your efforts with ours so that we can complete the construction of the X11 prototype by August 19. Specifically, I want to know if you will be able to complete the design of the fuselage by the agreed-upon target date of May 6. I have to have your answer by February 20, because our completion strategy depends on knowing as accurately as possible when your part of the project will be finished.

I do want to emphasize that we are more interested in quickly getting an accurate estimate of a completion date than in meeting the original target date of May 6.

A prompt reply would therefore be much appreciated.

_____

_____

_____

_____

_____

If you are working through this book on your own, you may score your Quiz according to the correct answers on page 200.

If not, your instructor will have the answers to the Quiz.

QUIZ FOR LESSON 6

NAME: _____ DATE:_____

Suppose you are the Credit Manager in the Credit Department of the Regent Pipe Company, Inc., a large manufacturer of steel, aluminum, and ceramic pipe and tubing. You have been reviewing financial statements and projections of the William F. Mauser Construction Company, Inc., which has applied to your firm for an increase in its credit line from $20,000 to $250,000 in a letter dated May 15 from Mrs. Pamela Carlisle, Vice President. The reason she wants the increase is that Mauser Construction has just won a million dollar contract from United Electric, a local utility company, to lay a seventy-mile gas line. Thus they estimate that they will need about $250,000 worth of 6″ steel pipe.

You have been familiar with Mauser Construction for several years and are confident that they have the experience and ability to complete such a project successfully. However, in going over their recent financial statements, you notice that the firm is already heavily in debt. In fact, total debt is about $500,000, while the net worth of the firm is only $600,000. Thus, if Regent Pipe sold Mauser $250,000 worth of pipe on credit, Mauser's total indebtedness would soar to $750,000—$150,000 more than the net worth. This would mean that Mauser's creditors would have more money invested in the firm than its owners—a very unhealthy situation for a business in the construction industry, which needs to be financially in sound order to have the flexibility to meet unexpected contingencies. Thus you must refuse to increase Mauser's credit line to $250,000.

In going over the contract between Mauser and the utility company, you note that it provides for a series of five progress payments of $200,000 each over the six months that the project is expected to last. You figure that if you allowed Mauser a credit line of $50,000 (i.e., they can purchase up to that amount of merchandise on credit), they could buy the pipe they need a little at a time. That way, total debt would not jump to such an unhealthy level right away. Instead, the income from the progress payments would allow Mauser to keep debt down as it went along.

Now jot down the ideas you want to include in your letter to Mrs. Carlisle, indicating your decision. Remember, you want to keep Mauser Construction as a customer.

_____   _____

_____   _____

_____   _____

_____   _____

_____

_____   _____

_____   _____

_____   _____

_____   _____

_____   _____

_____   _____

Go over your list of ideas. Cross out any that are irrelevant. Which ones will you use in your opening? Your closing? Now, on a separate sheet of paper, write a *draft* of your letter to Mrs. Carlisle and edit it to make it clear, concise, well-organized, natural, courteous, and personal. Then copy your letter in the spaces provided below. Your letter should now be in polished form, ready for mailing.

Dear Mrs. Carlisle:

_____

_____

_____

_____

_____

_____

_____

_____

_____

_____

_____

_____

_____

_____

_____

_____

_____

_____

_____

_____

_____

_____

_____

_____

_____

_____

_____

_____

_____

_____

If you are working through this book on your own, you may score your Quiz according to the correct answers on page 202.

If not, your instructor will have the answers to the Quiz.

ANSWERS FOR DIAGNOSTIC TEST

Below are the answers for the Diagnostic Test. Deduct the indicated number of points for each incorrect answer.

For items 1–4, the following ten faults should have been corrected:

		Points
1.	of the fact that	10
2.	about five or six	10
3.	personally feel	10
4.	along the lines that	10
5.	under date	10
6.	which is located	10
7.	purposes	10
8.	at an early date	10
9.	In order	10
10.	basic fundamentals	10
	TOTAL:	100

A score of 60 or less for items 1–4 indicates that Lesson 1 should be completed.

1. Our operators were not able to complete some long distance calls because ~~of the fact that~~ transmission cables were out at about five ~~or six~~ of our installations.

    or

    . . . at about ~~five or~~ six of our installations.

    or

    . . . at ~~about~~ five or six of our installations.

2. I ~~personally~~ feel that our advertising campaign should be designed ~~along~~

        as

~~the lines that~~ I outlined in my letter ~~under date~~ of March 22.

        ∧

3. Our factory ~~which is located~~ in Bellevue has been shut down for retooling

                                        soon, quickly, etc.

~~purposes~~ but should begin producing again ~~at an early date~~.
                                                  ^

4. ~~In order~~ to receive your certificate, you must complete a course on the ~~basic~~ fundamentals of cost accounting.

    or

                 basics

. . . on the ~~basic fundamentals~~ of cost accounting.
             ^

For items 5–7, the following five general words should have been underlined:

		Points
1.	was achieved	10
2.	measurable change	10
3.	worthwhile	10
4.	get in contact with	10
5.	to effect	10

For items 8–12, the following should have been done:

	Points
Item 8 should be checked (5 points) and revised into an active sentence (5 points).	10
Item 9 should *not* be checked or revised.	10
Item 10 should *not* be checked or revised.	10
Item 11 should be checked (5 points) and revised into an active sentence (5 points).	10
Item 12 should be checked (5 points) and revised into an active sentence (5 points).	<u>10</u>
TOTAL:	100

A score of 60 or less for items 5–12 indicates that Lesson 2 should be completed.

5. A 6 percent increase in sales *was achieved* in the Western District.

6. In May, there was a *measurable change* in the weather, indicating that the cloud-seeding program may have been *worthwhile*.

     7. When you reach Amarillo, our regional representative will *get in contact with* you and try *to effect* a reconcilement of your accounts.

√ 8. This shipment to us was received on June 10.

       We received this shipment on June 10.

_____ 9. Mr. McGraw is the first employee to receive benefits under our new company health-care plan.

_____ 10. I will phone you as soon as the job is finished by the consultant.

√ 11. Diversification of our product line was delayed by lack of capital.

       Lack of capital delayed diversification of our product line.

√ 12. You may be assured that I will give you all the help I can.

       I assure you that I will give you all the help I can.

For items 13–17, the following answers are correct:

		Points
13.	and	10
14.	for	10
15.	however, nevertheless	10
16.	Consequently, Therefore	10
17.	or	10

For items 18–22, the following should have been done:

	Points
Item 18 should be checked (5 points) and the mistake in parallelism corrected (5 points).	10
Item 19 should *not* be checked or revised.	10
Item 20 should be checked (5 points) and the mistake in parallelism corrected (5 points).	10
Item 21 should be checked (5 points) and the mistake in parallelism corrected (5 points).	10
Item 22 should be checked (5 points) and the mistake in parallelism corrected (5 points).	10
TOTAL:	100

A score of 60 or less for items 13–22 indicates that Lesson 3 should be completed.

___✓___ 18. I wanted not only *to find* out what went wrong but also *to ask* the manager to assure us that it would not happen again.

or

I not only *found out* what went wrong but also *asked* the manager to assure us that it would not happen again.

_____ 19. You may choose Plan A, which is less costly, but more inconvenient, or Plan B, which is more costly but less inconvenient.

___✓___ 20. This offer had a twofold purpose—*to stimulate* dealer sales and *to educate* individual customers.

or

This offer had a twofold purpose—*the stimulation of* dealer sales and *the education of* individual customers.

___✓___ 21. All our operatives are given instruction in *handling investigations* and *analyzing data.*

or

All our operatives are given instruction on *how to handle investigations* and *(how) to analyze data.*

___✓___ 22. *To stimulate* higher gross sales is not necessarily *to make* a higher profit.

or

Stimulating higher gross sales is not necessarily *making* a higher profit.

For items 23–26, the following revisions should have been made.

Points

23. After ~~Subsequent to~~ our meeting, I had a long talk   10

with Mr. Abrams ~~with reference to~~ about, concerning your   10

application and ~~regret to inform you~~ am sorry to say, etc. that he   10
did not approve it.

24. If ~~In the event that~~ the assignment is completed   10

satisfactorily, I will send you a bill ~~pursuant~~ as we   10

~~to our agreement of~~ agreed on May 10.

25. ~~It is impossible for delivery of the~~ We would be happy to deliver your station

wagon ~~to be made until~~ about a week after

Christmas.   10

26. ~~Enclosed herewith please find~~ Here is, I am enclosing, etc. a new contract,   10

which you should ~~duly note~~ read, study,   10

~~affix your signature thereto~~ sign,   10

and return to ~~this office~~ me, us.   <u>10</u>

TOTAL: 100

If a score of 60 or less was made for items 23–26, Lesson 4 should be completed.

For items 27–35, below are the correct answers.

		Points
27.	no	10
28.	To tell the reader what your letter is about.	10
29.	the reader	10
30.	no	10
31.	Referring to the date of the reader's letter makes it easier for her or him to identify it in the files.	10
32.	no	10
33.	you	10
34.	yes	10
35.	a. Request action from the reader.	10
	b. Summarize what has been said in the body of the letter.	10
	TOTAL:	100

If a score of 60 or less was made for items 27–35, Lesson 5 should be completed.